blackberry juice

blackberry juice

by

RALPH C. HAMM III

FIRST EDITION

Little Red Cell Publishing
New London, Connecticut. 06320

First Edition, 2015, manufactured in USA
1 2 3 4 5 6 7 8 9 10   LSI   20 19 18 17 16 15

Set in Bleeding Cowboys, Arial, Perpetua, New Times Roman, and Trajan Pro

Photograph of Ralph Conrad Hamm used by kind permission of the author.

Front cover photograph of the lynching of Thomas Shipp and Abram Smith (1930, Indiana), is by Lawrence H. Beitler who died in 1974. The photograph of the prisoners is by unknown author and in the public domain. The photograph of the USA flag is in the public domain. Front cover illustration by Annie Zimanski.

Book Layout and Cover Design:
Michael J Linnard, MCSD

Library of Congress Cataloging-in-Publication Data:

Hamm, Ralph Conrad.
  Blackberry Juice / by Ralph Conrad Hamm III. -- 1st ed.
    p. cm.
  ISBN 978-1-935656-37-1 (pbk. : alk. paper)
  I. Poetry. II. American Politics III. Prison Reform. Title.
  PS3623.O664S93 2015
  811'.6--dc22

Little Red Cell Publishing
[Imprint of Little Red Tree Publishing]
New London, Connecticut, USA
www.littleredcell.com

DEDICATION

This book is dedicated to those in pursuit of critical consciousness and thought, by way of higher education, as the means to forward the cause of liberation.

ACKNOWLEDGEMENT

I wish to acknowledge the Metropolitan College of Boston University and their prisoner education program; as well as the generosity of the Boston University Alumni and contributors, who have correctly gauged the correlation between higher education and successful prisoner re-entry into mainstream society, as being the bulwark against prisoner recidivism.

SPECIAL THANKS TO Professors Jennifer Drew, Karen Lischinsky, Gary Donato, Anne Blackwill, Jill McDonough, Paul Pelan, Kaia Stern, Patrick Dempsey, Jeffrey Racioppi, and the late Dante Germanotta; all of whom have left an indelible impression upon my critical consciousness via higher education.

To the warrior...the priest...the comrade-in-arms...Father Russell Carmichael, who had the vision (along with Arnie Coles, Dave Collins, and Stanley Jones) to reform the Massachusetts correctional system in the late nineteen-sixties. His vision soon led to a reform movement that birthed both the New England Prisoners' Association and the National Prisoners' Reform Association in the early nineteen-seventies. Today, he operates a homeless refuge for the socially marginalized poor and disenfranchised in New London, Connecticut. To the guardian angel.

CONTENTS

FOREWORD

Blackberry Juice is an impressive collection of short stories, essays, poetry, and a play, from a remarkable man who has spent the greater part of his life in prison. It is the third book Little Red Cell has published by Ralph C. Hamm III, as he enters his 47th year of imprisonment. It contains a wide range of his writing styles that not only attest to his talent as a writer but also to his insight, vision, and intellect as a black leader of stature in the prison reform movement and the black community in general.

It is to be expected that a prisoner, in their 47th year—having entered when just 17—might focus and return time and time again to the circumstances surrounding their continued imprisonment. However, this iteration is amply offset but the variety of form and contexts. Ralph explores his life journey directly via autobiographical short stories, the analytical essay form and through artistic forms of poetry and a play.

When I first received this manuscript I was in awe of the many powerfully written pieces that dealt with the inherent racism of the society that Ralph grew up in and the injustices both past, present and future that have been visited upon him and the black community, in Massachusetts specifically and in America generally. I thought long and hard about the best arrangement of these diverse forms and finally decided to rearrange the original sequence so that there would be a poetic prologue and epilogue—book ends if you will—grouping all other forms of writing into chapters, so that the reader might easily move from one to the other. With this presentation the reader can thus savor his poetry, short stories, political writing and play writing... all in one book.

However, there is no avoiding the intensity of this writing nor the integrity of this author, from the Prologue to the Epilogue, from the first chapter, where Ralph defines why he writes at all, to the last chapter, a powerfully written play of the reality of prison life.

Although Ralph provided an original piece of artwork for the front cover—it actually appears in his book, *Dear Stranger / The Wayfarer (2014)*—I decided that it did not fully capture the enormity of the concept of the book. The title, *Blackberry Juice*, although in one sense innocuous and innocent, is to my mind a powerful euphemism for the darkness that sits at the heart of America. It does not avoid the harsh multi-generational truth—oppression, racism, bigotry and injustice of black people in America from its founding to the present—and I chose to visually portray the full dimension. I maintained the original concept of racism, with all its unspeakable manifestations in US history, but distilled into the vision of people—their lives, hopes, dreams and future—being crushed in a clenched fist: a death grip and rendered into juice that pours into jars... sealed, imprisoned. I added a map where these jars were scattered all over the United States. This completed illustration, by Anne Zimanski, is superimposed upon a backdrop of two photographs. The top is the iconic photograph of the lynching of Thomas Shipp and Abram Smith, in Marion, Indiana, on August 7, 1930, taken by Lawrence H. Beitler. This photograph was the inspiration for Abel Meeropol to write a poem "Strange Fruit" who later turned it into a song and most famously sung by Billie Holiday. The photograph at the bottom is a typical image of the mass incarceration of young black men you might see in any number of prisons throughout American.

Blackberry Juice is a powerful book, not a palliative full of mellifluous words attempting to soften the implications of these harsh truths, too often ignored or simply dismissed as the contumelious ranting of an "angry black man," merely playing the "race card," rather it is a clear-eyed, analytical expose, by a gifted writer, of the realities and implications of racism for one prisoner who is in need of justice. A justice, it is hoped, to which this book might contribute in a small measure, so that I may one day personally hand a copy to the author, as a free man.

Michael Linnard
New London, CT, 2015

INTRODUCTION

"Lighting is flashing outside the windows, and a torrent of rain falls. It is about midnight and everyone has quit, as they always do during a hunger strike. It is my time to stretch out and relax. I've lead these prisoners, all 755, to raise their voices in peaceful protest against the Massachusetts Prison System. I am their leader, their representative, the designated Camp Chairman. In the dark silence I pray none of us gets hurt."

(Father Russell Carmichael, Founder NPRA)

How many years has it been? How long and hard a struggle? It did not start out that way. Like all prisoners I was sentenced for wrongdoing. I deserved to go to prison for the crimes I committed. Nevertheless, three years into my sentence the treatment I received, or lack of it, turned me into a victim. Something was wrong and I was not one to stay "quit" and not do something about my condition.

I had an advantage over other prisoner's. I was a leader who had a very powerful group of followers. I was somewhat educated, came from a solid family and had political connections. The prison administrators just wanted me to shut up, do my time and get out quietly. It was not meant to happen.

In the late 1960s, in the jails and prisons of Massachusetts, members of my own crew, and other convicted prisoners, were beginning to become educated and recruited to form peaceful united groups to protest and rebel against an oppressively unfair prison system that made victims out of sentenced criminals.

Ralph Hamm III, was one of those recruits: a young teenager of Seventeen, sentenced to natural life. By the time I was introduced to Ralph he had already come under the wing of my associate, Robert

Dellelo, another of our prison leaders, and a part of our greater coalition of activism. Along with my partner, Arnie Coles, we introduced Ralph to the struggles of the political prisoner, molding him through education and the unity of camaraderie into a warrior for our civil rights struggle. Little did we know then, how far and how articulate he would carry our struggle. My love for Ralph Hamm is united with the love for Dave Collins, Stanley Jones, Arnie, though passed on, lives in our hearts and minds, with dedication and loyalty that is only molded in men who fight in foxholes together, we covered each others back from harms way; no words can adequately describe nor explain that life time bond.

Our vision carries on through Ralph and his work; though we left him in the cage, in the "Belly of the Beast," he carried on from the New England Prisoners Association to our dream of the first Prisoners Union in the Country (NPRA) hope is carried on through, Ralph Hamm III, my brother warrior.

This book of poetry, short stories, a play, and essays, is his story—our story—in which he articulates the pain of suffering like few can. He is a tall, strong, black leader. He is a Stokely Carmichael, a Malcolm X and a Cornel West all rolled up into one. Members of the Massachusetts parole board described his writing as "angry." One past chairman of the board actually told him to "die in prison." I see no anger in Ralph's writing, deep frustration most certainly yes; in fact I wonder how any black man, brought up in the most oppressive society, as it relates to its justice system and one of undying racism, could not be angry or frustrated. My white privilege allowed me to leave my friend behind for the last forty-seven years. I pray he will be released, be free; he did not kill anyone; it is a fact that older men, involved in his crime, used him as the scapegoat; a kid to be used and then thrown away.

I sometimes wonder how much our influence lead to Ralph having to serve our time, as retribution or payment to the oppressive prison system for our being the kind of fools who faced Caesar and his starving lions. As Jack Henry Abbott would say: all we had to do was walk away, do our time, retract a statement, and suppress the "'fuck you' to Caesar" Knowing full well the consequences, we were and remain men that just could not do that.

I have been a leader in the Prison reform movement now for over fifty years. I do not stop. Ralph does not stop. The phrase, often spoken by all of us in prison reform, for as long as I can remember and still stands: "While one is chained, I am not free." Few men in our country have borne the lash of the Justice System like Ralph C Hamm III. It is a story that needs to be told. Listen to his words. Feel the bars that hold his voice.

Father Russell Carmichael
New London, CT 2015

PROLOGUE

BLACKBERRY JUICE

Those stains upon your hands,
and up under your nails,
are not there by chance—
they were obtained quite deliberately.

For, in your quest to seize
the nectar, some tried to escape
in a desperate and frantic
attempt to be free.

Once clinging to the ancestral bush,
from where others before
had been plucked, to thereby gain
the status of delicacy...
our young unripened fruit
are canned to preserve their texture
and flavor, to sate the hunger
and thirst of a cannibalistic society.

As your unrelinquishing grip
squeezes me tighter
I plead for release,
but what is the use.

My pulpy body, and syrupy soul
have been rendered apart. Now I seep
through your fingers
and run down your arm
    like wild blackberry juice.

This poem is a revised version of "Preserves," which was first published in Dear Stranger / The Wayfarer *(1979), and reprinted in a new edition by Little Red Cell Publishing in (2014).*

Chapter I

Why Do I Write?

WHY DO I WRITE?
WHAT DO I WRITE ABOUT?

Why do I write?

I write because a prison needs a poet—a chronicler—someone who has experienced at firsthand the agony of the disenfranchised, and can interpret through his very soul the expression of suffering by the collective whole.

I write because the only way for the public to learn about what it is like to sub-exist within "the bowels of the beast" (the criminal justice system) is to listen to an inhabitant. Not just any inhabitant, but one who understands and can articulate the conditions of his confinement. No criminal psychologist, sociologist, so-called criminal justice professional, nor salaried correctional official knows what it is truly like to venture through the looking-glass of the criminal justice system as a member of the marginalized under-caste in America—unless they have served time themselves.

I write because the Massachusetts Parole Board has told me, after having served over 40 years on a non-capital life sentence, to die in prison because of my beliefs.

I write because I refuse to quietly go to my grave.

I write because my life was offered as a sacrifice upon the altar of criminal justice: as the means to secure and uphold an easy and speedy conviction—to curry favor and gratitude from a race-conscious and vindictive society—to secure a method in the Commonwealth to undermine the Constitutional guarantees to trial by jury and effective assistance of trial counsel...and to forward the careers of those involved with the so-called professional aspects of the case in the Massachusetts legal system.

I write because criminal justice in Massachusetts is told as a one-sided story: where voices of the poor under-caste are seldom, if ever, heard...where there are no second chances, nor room for redemption.

I write because in Massachusetts the courts have declared that it is "reasonable" for skin color to be the determinant factor in coercing juvenile defendants to waive trial by jury—that trial counsel does not have to investigate the facts of a criminal case if he has access to the prosecutor's case file, in spite of the Massachusetts Canon of Ethics— and, as a result, that physical, material, and exculpatory evidence can be withheld or destroyed prior to trial.

I write because juvenile first time offenders, such as myself, can receive life sentences for non capital offenses, because he is "black and his victims white" ...that an adult codefendant, and ringleader of said criminal episode, can enter into a secret sentencing deal with the Commonwealth, testify against and inculcate a juvenile codefendant, and thereby be released from charges against a female victim and returned to the community to commit even more egregious crimes... that victims can be convinced to lie, without having to face cross-examination from trial counsel, because counsel has determined that the victims have been through enough already.

I write because it is the desire of the criminal justice system to have its victims suffer in obscurity, to be tortured away from prying eyes and a possible scrutiny by the mass media; thereby absolving society from any plausible charge of injustice, as well as from the realization that the social conditions that birth criminal behavior are responsible for crime.

I write because America is a country whose social reality is viewed by most through the prism of rose-tinted glasses, after first being distorted by a series of Fun House mirrors and smokescreens...a society where the Voters' Rights Act of 1965 and 1970 must be continually renewed by a sitting President, in an effort to guarantee that black people (the descendants of slaves) maintain their right to vote...a country where one of the by-products of mass incarceration, in several states, is a lifetime of disenfranchisement of the right to vote and the methodology utilized by politicos to circumvent the Voters' Rights Acts.

I write because in spite of America's bombast proclaiming freedom and liberty for all, the 13th Amendment to the U.S. Constitution holds an authorized exception to the abolition of slavery, which is rigidly enforced and exploited.

I write because.

What do I write about?

I write about how the Massachusetts criminal justice system is criminal to the degree where it is not a system of justice, it is a system of "just-us." The system is designed to fool enough of the general public, enough of the time to justify its disparities against racial minorities and the poor. It is a system of "just-us" that reserves its severest penalties and sentences for its lower income/caste members of society, except when the violations of the law are bartered with informants and/or members of organized crime tendered by a rose in a fisted kid glove.

For example, I write about: in what other system of social control can a black juvenile first time offender receive a life sentence for intending to commit a crime, as well as receive a consecutive life sentence for his involvement in a $20.00 robbery of an emphasized white person, and thereby serve over 46 years in prison: while a white organized crime hit-man can confess to killing 18 people, barter and serve only 12 years in prison, and be released back into society as an avowed serial killer; and the black juvenile's trial/defense attorney (as a white member of yet another aspect of organized crime in this State) can rob a client of $100,000.00 from an estate, barter, and not serve one minute in prison.

I write about the benefits of the criminal "just-us" system serving as an economic advantage for the middle and upper castes, and the social institutions at work to maintain rather than eliminate crime—to reinforce the levels of caste in society. Why must crime be maintained? It is essential to have a visible (black) criminal population as a boundary by which to establish a cultural identity in society, and to sustain a solidarity amongst those who share that cultural identity. Criminal "just-us" is nothing more than a system of perpetual regulations and mirages used to marginalize the disenfranchised poor as scapegoats for society's shortcomings.

Chapter II

PAROLE BOARD 2014

Opening Statement
&
Decision
&
Response

RALPH C. HAMM III

OPENING STATEMENT

SEPTEMBER 9, 2014,
PAROLE ELIGIBILITY HEARING

I will open my brief statement by attempting to explain why I do not have any community support in attendance at this hearing. My support group have stood beside me for over the past 15 years to no avail. Many of them were emotionally shaken as a result of my September 15, 2009 parole eligibility hearing when it was learned that there is the possibility that I will die in prison because of my beliefs. I have come to realize over the course of four and a half decades that my version of the crime does not matter…that "remorse" means not committing crime, and not creating new victims. However, what does matter is the victims' understanding of what happened to them and why it happened. I thereby came to realize, after listening closely to my supporters' understanding of what happened to them and why, that I was in essence enabling the creation of new victims by asking my family and friends to support me at parole eligibility hearings. So, I asked them not to attend anymore.

It has become obvious to me that the truth of my life experience and survival will always be unfathomable to anyone who has not personally undertaken a similar journey. My life experience, and what I have found to be necessary for my continued growth and survival, will often be at odds with what someone, who does not really know me, thinks about me and what I need. A cookie cutter approach to reality never works. People are uniquely individual. Today is not 1968, when I was a juvenile and my crimes were committed, nor is it 1970s Walpole State Prison where I grew into adulthood within the most violent prison per Capita in America. It would be a mistake to become transfixed upon those bygone eras for the purpose of trying to define who I am. I am not the 17 year old adolescent in the woods motivated by fright and relying upon my baser primal instincts…I am not in my early twenties besieged on all sides and depending upon my anger and aggression to mask my fears in an effort to stay alive in a hostile prison environment. I am an

9

educated and, I would like to believe, rational 63 year old adult who has managed to survive 45 years of imprisonment the best way that I could given the circumstances, while serving non capital first offenses that were committed when I was a teenager.

In a little over 2 months time I will turn 64 years of age, and I have essentially forfeited my entire life for the harm caused to Kathleen McGrath and Raymond Gagnon—the two initial victims of the 1968 criminal episode.

3-1

The Commonwealth of Massachusetts
Executive Office of Public Safety
PAROLE BOARD
12 Mercer Road
Natick, Massachusetts 01760

Charles D. Baker
Governor

Karyn Polito
Lieutenant Governor

Daniel Bennett
Secretary

Telephone # (508) 650-4500
Facsimile # (508) 650-4599

Charlene Bonner
Chairperson

Janis DiLoreto Smith
Executive Director

received a copy of the Record of Decision on 3-3-15 witness ___ Ferten LPO MCI-Norfolk

DECISION

IN THE MATTER OF

RALPH HAMM

W32301

TYPE OF HEARING:	Review Hearing
DATE OF HEARING:	September 9, 2014
DATE OF DECISION:	February 26, 2015

PARTICIPATING BOARD MEMBERS: Dr. Charlene Bonner, Tonomey Coleman, Sheila Dupre, Tina Hurley, Lucy Soto-Abbe

DECISION OF THE BOARD: After careful consideration of all relevant facts, including the nature of the underlying offense, criminal record, institutional record, the inmate's testimony at the hearing, and the views of the public as expressed at the hearing or in written submissions to the Board, we conclude by unanimous vote that the inmate is not a suitable candidate for parole. Parole is denied with a review in five years.

I. STATEMENT OF THE CASE

On June 27, 1969, after a bench trial, Ralph Hamm was found guilty of two counts of armed robbery, two counts of mayhem, and one count each of assault with intent to rape and assault with intent to kill. He received two concurrent life sentences and several sentences ordered to run from and after the life sentences that were later reduced by the Appellate Division of the Superior Court.[1]

---

[1] "As reduced, the sentences are as follows: Terms of life imprisonment, to be served concurrently, were imposed for the armed robbery of [Victim B] and assault with intent to rape her. Upon completion of service of those sentences, the following sentences will come into effect, consecutively: fifteen to twenty years for the armed robbery of [Victim A]; two and one-half to five years for the mayhem on him; two and one-half to five years for the mayhem on [Victim B]; and six to ten years for the assault with intent to kill her, for a total term of imprisonment of life, to be followed by a term of twenty-six to forty years." *Commonwealth v. Ralph C. Hamm*, 19 Mass. App. Ct. 72, 81 n. 1 (1984).

1

The facts are culled from the Massachusetts Appeals Court decision denying his motion for a new trial. *Commonwealth v. Ralph C. Hamm*, 19 Mass.App.Ct. 72 (1984). On November 23, 1968, Victim A, a male, and Victim B, a female,[2] were parked in a wooded area of Lawrence. It was in this area, at approximately 1:00 am, when the couple was attacked inside their vehicle by Ralph Hamm, then 17 years old, Robert Preston, and Emanuel Smith. After rocking the car, the men opened the driver's door and dragged Victim A from the vehicle, punching and beating him about the face until he lost consciousness. Victim B was also dragged out of the vehicle. She was beaten and stripped of her clothing. After the beating, an eleven inch branch was forced into her vagina to the point of perforating her abdominal cavity. Victim A, who had been unconscious, awoke to see the three men leaving the scene after setting the couple's car on fire. Evidence presented at the trial revealed that it was Ralph Hamm who thrust the tree branch into the Victim B's vagina.

II. INSTITUTIONAL/CRIMINAL HISTORY

Ralph Hamm's criminal history began with the heinous crimes he committed the night of November 23, 1968. Subsequently, in 1971, he was convicted of assault on a correctional officer and sentenced to one year to one year and a day to be served from and after his current life sentence. He also received a three to five year concurrent sentence for assault and battery with a dangerous weapon, which is a crime he committed while incarcerated.

Ralph Hamm had a poor adjustment to incarceration in his early years, as he engaged in violent and assaultive behavior. He would fight and threaten inmates and correctional staff. Throughout the 1970's and into the 1980's, Hamm continued to experience difficulty adjusting to prison life. His behavior included fighting, being disruptive, using obscene language, threatening staff members, disobeying orders, and being insolent. Hamm's behavior improved throughout the 1980's and 1990's and he has only incurred five discipline reports since 1990. His last violation was in 2007, which was for being out of place and being disruptive.

Hamm earned his high school equivalency diploma in Walpole in 1973, continued to pursue his education, and graduated from Bunker Hill Community College with an Associate's Degree in Liberal Arts in 1986. In 1999, he became a Certified Legal Assistant through the Blackstone School of Law. Between 2002 and 2004, he earned three diplomas from The College of Divine Metaphysics. In 2012, Hamm graduated Magna Cum Laude in Liberal Studies from Boston University's Metropolitan College. In June 2014, he earned a diploma from the Prisoner Assistance Scholastic Service (PASS) in Personal Psychological Development. During Hamm's incarceration, he became a prolific writer and had some of his works published. If paroled, Hamm hopes to continue his education in a graduate program. Since his last parole hearing, he has completed numerous programs relevant to his rehabilitation. He is currently unemployed at MCI-Norfolk. He stated that he is employed at The Little Red Cell Publishing Company as a writer and editor.

III. PAROLE HEARING ON SEPTEMBER 9, 2014

This is Hamm's fourth time before the Parole Board. His most recent hearing was in 2009, when he received a denial with the maximum five year review. The Parole Board asked

---

[2] The Board will use pseudonyms to identify the victims. See G.L. c. 265 § 24C, the "Rape Shield law."

Hamm about his last hearing and his understanding of why he was denied. Hamm stated that he was "emotionally shaken because of the last hearing." He stated that since the hearing, he came to the realization that he may die in prison. He also stated that he did not want any of his supporters to attend this hearing, as he felt that he was "creating new victims." Hamm insisted that he was not treated well by the Parole Board and did not agree with its decision. Hamm stated that he has been incarcerated for 45 years and is not a danger to society, but rather a success story for the Department of Correction.

The Parole Board questioned Hamm regarding previous recommendations that he engage in the Sex Offender Treatment Program (SOTP). Given the vicious sexual assault that he has been convicted of, the Parole Board conveyed that there is a significant concern that he has not addressed this portion of the crime. In fact, Hamm has distanced himself from the sexual victimization of the crime. Hamm maintained that he did not sexually assault the victim with a stick or in any other way. He acknowledged, however, that he has been convicted of participating in the sexual offense. Hamm then explained that although he engaged in SOTP, he did not benefit, nor did he need, such treatment due to the mandates of the program and the risk assessments that are used. Hamm also stated that he was considered to be "a fighter" because he questioned many aspects of the program. Thus, he was in jeopardy of being terminated. Hamm provided several examples as to why the program was not valid and stated that he terminated it on his own. In addition, Hamm cited details in prior police reports that supported his version of the offense. One Board Member asked Hamm why he admitted to details that constituted a sexual offense when he was engaged in SOTP. Hamm stated, "The reason why I said that to her (staff) was because, at the time, I was under the impression I had to admit that to get through the program." When asked if any part of the program was helpful, he stated, "I've assisted them (the staff) more than they assisted me." When asked if he would be willing to engage in SOTP again, now that the program has been revised, he stated that he has heard the SOTP program has changed, but acknowledged that he had other priorities, specifically in pursuing his education, as opposed to re-engaging in SOTP. However, throughout the hearing, Hamm maintained that he did not commit a sexual offense.

The Parole Board questioned Hamm on his version of the offense. According to a cooperating witness regarding the crimes for which he was convicted of, Hamm continues to present a conflicting version. One Member of the Parole Board reminded Hamm that throughout the years, no one has believed his version. This places Hamm in a difficult position since it calls into question his level of rehabilitation. Hamm acknowledged the conflict and stated that he understands his conviction. He also understands that he would have to comply with the recommendations of the Parole Board in order to be seriously considered for parole. The Parole Board questioned Hamm on some controversial statements that he wrote in one of his books. He was asked if those writings would be viewed by the public as someone who is ready to cooperate and transition back to society. He explained that the passages that were called into question were related to "what happened in the '70's. I was trying to be honest about how I felt in the '70's." He was asked if he had a different perspective now versus some of his published opinions in 2008. Hamm stated, "All of it. I have new books that will show that. The changes described are a result of maturity, change in circumstances, meditation, and education." Hamm stated that his writings are a great source of his rehabilitation.

Hamm stated that he has progressed in his rehabilitation and has moved beyond his prior behavior and reputation as being "a fighter." He said that he has committed himself to his

3

writing and works with a publisher for a stipend of $100 per month. Hamm's writings include issues of social justice and political essays. He stated that he is currently writing a collection of short stories and that he is working on his memoir. Hamm also stated that he has completed numerous programs related to all aspects of his rehabilitation and that he is not 17 years-old anymore. He stated that, "I've done enough time, even if I did every crime they said." He said that he has addressed all of those issues and that he came into the prison system during a violent period in the state prison system. He emphasized that he has progressed from an angry young boy to a 63 year-old man who is not a threat to society. Hamm stated that he maintains a close support system and outlined a parole plan that includes living with his long-time companion, continuing his writing career, engaging in mental health counseling, and obtaining computer training. Hamm stated that he has identified two job opportunities. He also reminded the Parole Board that he had approximately 20 supporters attend his last hearing, but asked them not to attend this hearing.

Speaking in opposition to Hamm's parole was Essex County Assistant District Attorney Catherine Semel. ADA Semel also provided a detailed written statement of opposition from the District Attorney's Office. In her testimony before the Parole Board, ADA Semel emphasized that Hamm has never accepted responsibility for the offenses that he committed. She stated that the victim of the sexual assault testified at his trial and identified Hamm as her assailant. ADA Semel also pointed to additional evidence that disputed Hamm's claims. ADA Semel concluded that Hamm has not committed to any meaningful rehabilitation and that he continued with litigation to alleviate his responsibility. On behalf of the District Attorney's Office, ADA Semel requested that the Parole Board deny Hamm's parole.

IV. DECISION

Ralph Hamm was convicted of several crimes, including armed robbery and assault with intent to rape. He received two concurrent life sentences that were aggregated with his several consecutive sentences to create an initial parole eligibility date of April 15, 1998.[3] These crimes relate to a vicious and sexually sadistic attack perpetrated by Hamm and two cohorts on a young woman and young man who, unfortunately, just happened to cross their paths that evening. Evidence presented at trial revealed that it was Hamm who thrust an eleven inch branch into the victim's vagina, perforating the female victim's abdominal cavity.

Despite serving 45 years in prison, Hamm has not completed SOTP and maintains that he did not commit any sexual offense. The Parole Board notes that Hamm has engaged in rehabilitative programs and his conduct has significantly improved throughout his incarceration. The Parole Board also commends Hamm for committing himself to higher education; however, Hamm has chosen to prioritize certain areas of rehabilitation that he deems of higher importance than others. The Parole Board verbalized concerns that Hamm has not come to terms with the offenses he committed, thus demonstrating a resistance to meaningful rehabilitation.

The standard we apply in assessing candidates for parole is set out in 120 C.M.R. 300.04, which provides that "Parole Board Members shall only grant a parole permit if they are of the opinion that there is a reasonable probability that, if such offender is released, the

---

[3] As Mr. Hamm's non-life sentences were for crimes committed *before* January 1, 1988, and were ordered to run consecutive to his life sentences, they were aggregated to create a single parole eligibility date.

4

offender will live and remain at liberty without violating the law and that release is not incompatible with the welfare of society." Applying that appropriately high standard here, it is the unanimous opinion of the Board that Hamm does not merit parole at this time because he is not rehabilitated. The review will be in five years, during which time Hamm should commit to a more comprehensive rehabilitation that addresses specific areas of need, including his lack of candor.

I certify that this is the decision and reasons of the Massachusetts Parole Board regarding the above referenced hearing. Pursuant to G.L. c. 127, § 130, I further certify that all voting Board Members have reviewed the applicant's entire criminal record. This signature does not indicate authorship of the decision.

_____   2/26/15
Jan/s DiLoreto Smith, Executive Director   Date

5

RALPH C HAMM III
RESPONSE TO PAROLE DECISION

It is hard to believe, but an irrefutable fact, that in 2015 the United States of America is the only country in the world that imprisons juvenile offenders [especially if they are black] to be tortured via a lifetime in prison, even if the original conviction was for a non capital first offense. I am such an offender, and have spent the past 46 years of my life in prison for a criminal episode that occurred when I was 17 years old [in 1968]. "Life" means natural life in Massachusetts jurisprudence, and for this first time juvenile offender there exists no true possibility of parole.

On February 26, 2015 the Massachusetts Parole Board insured that I will, in all probably, die in prison by mandating a further five year review for parole in my case—or when I reach 70 years of age. Their decision in part rests upon a profound dislike of my beliefs [convictions]. Consequently during the course of my September 9, 2014 parole eligibility hearing the contents of my 2012 published book, *Manumission: The Liberated Consciousness of a Prison(er) Abolitionist* was called into question, and was specifically referred to within the Board's 2015 decision.

The Parole Board contends that my book is "angry." They use the euphemistic phrase "… some controversial statements" in the actually final written decision [printing in full pages 3 - 5]. I, of course, contend that the book is not anger, but rather is a true historical account of the past, present, and possible future as pertains to the struggle for human rights by people of color and the marginalized poor in this Commonwealth. Self evidently my book has the capacity to bring forth anger and frustration in those readers who must feel a sense of guilt for their direct role or acquiescence in the repression of the political under caste in society, as said readers refuse to confront their own reflection in the pages. It is much easier to vilify the author than it is to face the truth, especially if the author is in prison. His truth can thereby be dismissed— written off—as his unqualified and contumelious anger.

But let us for argument's sake say that my writing is angry. Who conceivably deserves to be more angrier than a man whose entire life has been sucked out of him by the vampire State due to his race, as fuel to perpetuate the criminal just-us apparatus? Is it not better and more appropriate for an author to express his feelings and frustration with words in a book? A book can convey a myriad of emotion, as well as explain any perceived harmful after-effects designed to keep the criminal just-us industry in motion as the major source of economic growth and employment in this country. The United States has literally become a nation of barbed wire, concrete enclosures, and steel.

My success in higher education and program completion outside of the auspices of the Department of Corrections was recognized by the Board, but paled in comparison to my non-compliance with a correctional program [Sex Offenders Treatment Program (SOTP)] designed to define who I am for the rest of my life. I emphatically reject that definition. In my case, this lack of "programming" was construed as an indicator of my perceived inability to be able to abide by the conditions and terms of a granted parole. However, some prisoners who have been deemed to be "programmed" do recidivate. In fact Massachusetts' declared low rate of prisoner recidivism has more to do with fewer paroles being granted, deportations, and those prisoners having been released from custody, after completing their sentence, simply leaving this draconian State, than it has to do with any notion of a successful public safety policy due to prisoner "programming."

I had two adult codefendants during my 1968 criminal episode who were released from their State charges over 20 years ago due to their successful motions for a new trial. In an affidavit in support of their motion for a new trial, one of the co-defendants, Emanuel E. Smith, wrote:

"I was initially arrested in New York City on November 26. I was taken by many police officers from Lawrence, Massachusetts and New York to the home of a friend of my co-defendant, Robert Preston. I saw Preston being hit. I was handcuffed and taken in a bathroom. I was threatened that I could be shot if I did not make a statement concerning the November incident. Finally, in complete terror, I told the officer what he wanted to know—that Ralph Hamm had assaulted the female victim."

The 21 year old ringleader, Emanuel, became the "cooperating" witness against me at my trial when the situation became difficult, as the above quote describes, he received a secret sentencing deal—leading to his release from prison in 1986—and as far as I know is currently serving a 60 year sentence in Maryland for an even more egregious crime. The female victim, Kathleen, testified at my trial in compliance with my codefendant's induced testimony.

My parole release has never been opposed by the victims of the crimes, as my continued imprisonment rests solely upon the transparent racist vindictiveness inherent within Massachusetts politricks.

In Massachusetts organized crime hit men can confess to 18 murders and never serve a day in prison for the crimes, and juvenile offenders sentenced to natural life in prison for murder [who may have stabbed their victims multiple times and tortured them] can receive unanimous "politically correct" parole release decisions, while those juvenile offenders servicing natural life in prison for other than capital murder can find no advocacy in the State in support of leniency because the issue is not in the media spotlight of political correctness.

The language "possibility of parole" held within the 2012 landmark Supreme Court of the United States decision of Miller versus Alabama has afforded the loophole for the Massachusetts Parole Board to write parole decisions that deny parole to particular juvenile offenders it deems political prisoners ad infinitum, and thereby torture the offender to death in prison without any outcry from the so-called legal professionals of the State.

My institutional record lists only four acts of physical violence dating back to the 1970s, when I initially entered prison as a first time juvenile offender with white victims. All four, when you review them in detail, were in self-defense: three against prison guards who covered their heads under white pillow cases as they physically assaulted prisoners and declaring themselves members of the Klu Klux Klan, and one against a prisoner who attacked me with a shovel. These forty-year-old disciplinary charges and convictions continue to be held up as a testament to a violent demeanor. When the violent acts against me stopped, my so-called violent demeanor ceased to exist in my prison file.

To my mind it is clear, black males, descendant of slaves in America, are vilified by the government and the media if they even attempt to defend themselves against pure racism. In recent examples, we have, "Don't shoot!", "Hands up!", and "I can't breathe!". We are expected to suffer and die in silence.[1]

Let me be frank, the amount of time that I was sentenced to serve in prison, as a first time juvenile offender, is of course disparate and the by-product of institutional racism immanent to the criminal just-us industry, but the underlying behavior that garnered the exorbitant sentencing rests squarely upon my shoulders. I do not deny this reality.

Blackberry Juice is designed to speak to many victims, and is a loud testament of how we have, in many ways, all been led to victimize ourselves.

It goes without saying that I will continue to express my convictions and beliefs pertaining to "Massissippi" mistreatment within my writings and my books, until the Commonwealth's determination that I "die in prison" for non capital first offenses as a juvenile becomes a reality.

Aluta continuaa!

Ralph C. Hamm III
Massasschusetts, 2015

Notes

1. I am condemned to die in a State where my alleged Constitutional right to appeal my conviction is used against me for parole consideration by the Essex County District Attorney's Office, because I am black and my victims were white. Compare; Dred Scott v. John Sandford, Howard (1857): where a black man has no rights that whites are bound by law to respect.

CHAPTER III

SHORT STORIES

A PROFILE OF MY FATHER

"He was out!", bellowed the animated voice of my father from the living room. "No he wasn't!", intoned my Uncle Edgar. "What, are you blind, Junior?" Junior was the name that my uncle and my grandmother used when addressing my father...that, or Juny, as he was second descended with the name Ralph—named after his father.

I did not venture into the living room where my father and his brother were watching the baseball game on the television, but was content to remain in my bedroom. I was amusing myself by playing with a huge, red plastic, fire truck that actually pumped water—one of the joys in my eight year old life that was a gift from my previous Christmas.

My father was an avid baseball fan, as was my uncle. It was a fanaticism that I did not share. This revelation came at the chagrin of Junior. I can still recall his voice, when he attempted to convince me to take an interest in his game, "Ralphy, baseball is a man's game." I would look up at him, unconvinced. "It's America's game, son."

Ralph Conrad Hamm, Junior was extremely fair-skinned, and could 'pass for white' due to his straight hair (what blacks referred to as 'good hair') and corresponding skin tone. Yet, to his credit, he flew into a rage whenever any white person regarded him as other than black. At six feet in height, and weighing in at approximately one hundred and ninety pounds, he was a force to be reckoned with when he became angry. My mother, all five feet five inches and one hundred and fifteen pounds of her, appeared to be the only individual who could calm him down during these rare occasions. Most of the time, however, he came across to me as being quite even tempered; although he struck an imposing figure, and cast fear, whenever I broke a family rule or acted up in school and my mother angrily said, "Wait until your father gets home!"

I do not recall any anticipatory feelings toward the prospect of seeing my first live baseball game, but I do remember being overjoyed at the promise of spending a day with my father—who worked two jobs to support our family (five sisters and mother) and seldom appeared to be home except on the weekends. One evening, when my father returned home from working his day job as a truck driver, he handed me a small baseball glove that appeared to have been designed to fit my small left hand. He handed me the tan glove accompanied by a broad smile on his face, and informed me that the glove was to allow me to catch baseballs that flew my way at the baseball park the next afternoon.

It was Saturday afternoon in May of 1959. The sun was bright, as were my spirits, and there was a slight nip in the air when my father and I made our way to our seats in the stands at Fenway Park. There appeared to be quite a few people at the game, and I recall noticing the number of children around my age who also carried baseball gloves. I pointed this fact out to my father, who just patted me on the head and smiled. Of these children with the gloves, none were black, and I failed to notice any black adults there to watch the game from the limited view afforded my eight-year-old body stature.

No baseballs came my way that day in Fenway, but what did fly in my direction was spit, popcorn, beer, empty cups, and racial epithets of: "nigger," "tar baby," "fudgecicle," "spook," and "coon"; hurled at me by white adults, and their children, in attendance. Initially, my father was spared the projectiles and insults because my tormentors had probably mistaken him for white like themselves. However, when he took me up in his arms and raced with me up the aisle to the exit, the same garbage was thrown in his direction along with the jeers of: "nigger lover," amidst maniacal laughter.

I looked up into my father's face, expecting to see anger or the fear that saturated my being, but he appeared to be outwardly calm... emotionless. He calmly placed me upon the front passenger-side seat of the Ford Country Squire station wagon, that served as the family car, and never said a word all the way home. Occasionally he looked over at me while he was driving, and reached out a hand to brush something (possibly popcorn) off of my clothing. The fact that he remained so calm had the impact of alleviating my fear, as I sat next to him on the front seat of the automobile until I was able to amuse myself by looking out of the side window at the cars we passed on the way home.

In light of my father's short fuse on the matter of race, his self control that day was extraordinary. At eight years old, I did not consider why he did not lash out at our tormentors at Fenway, but today I can only assume that he did not want his true emotions to erupt and possibly endanger his young son. I never had the opportunity to ask him what was going through his mind then, because by the time that I reached the age where race became a serious concern for me as a teenager, and I could actually formulate the right question, he and my mother had parted company through divorce.

Spring evolved into summer...1959 flowed into 1962, as I grew into puberty. My father spent many weekend afternoons sitting in his lounger in the living room watching television, with a beer can in his hands. Uncle Edgar no longer came by the house, and I never noticed my father watching another major league baseball game; nor did he mention the sport of baseball to me again after the eventful afternoon of May 1959 in Fenway Park.

Later in my life, when I was in my twenties, I began my studies in African-American history. I came to learn that Jackie Robinson approached the Red Sox in 1945, at Fenway Park, seeking a spot on their team roster. It is recorded, as well as substantiated by both my parents in 1959, that Red Sox owner Tom Yawkey was to have yelled, "Get those niggers off my field!", once he noticed Robinson and two other black ball players standing at home plate.

What happened to my father and me in 1959 was the legacy of Fenway Park. To this day, at the age of sixty-two, I despise the game of baseball and the Boston Red Sox, in particular. I consciously equate the Red Sox insignia as a symbol of racism, similar to the cross of the Ku Klux Klan.

SPIRITS OF A DREAM

It is June 1972, and I am 21 years of age. I am hurriedly walking down the main corridor of Walpole State Prison in Massachusetts, on my way to the prison library. It is the six o'clock movement in the prison, where the convicts have ten minutes to journey from their respective cellblocks to a specific destination in the prison where they have signed out to go. The corridor is full of men like bees in a hive attempting to make their way to the gym, the yard, chapel, or wherever in the complex.

I enter the door of the library, and am confronted by greetings from the eleven black prisoners seated behind long wooden tables in the library-proper. We are assembled for our weekly session in African-American history. I take a seat, and face the course instructor - David Dance.

David is in his mid to late twenties, medium height, thin, light skinned black male, who sports a short afro style hairdo, and maintains a light goatee on his face. Today, he is wearing a light green short-sleeved sport shirt that is spreading a greyish looking Rorscharch pattern of sweat across his back, which I find tempting to interpret. Although there are three poled floor fans struggling to cool the area that the class is occupying, summer is not having any of it. The fans serve only to blow hot air from one side of the room to the other. It is so hot that even the library books, which fill the five tier high navy blue metal book shelves that separate the aisles of the library's floor space, appear to be oppressed by the heat. I swear that the two flies that have come to rest inert upon the table in front of me are sweating!

We were in our second month of studies with David. In January of this year he had approached the first black Commissioner of Corrections, John O. Boone, and requested that he be allowed to teach a comprehensive African-American history course in Walpole State Prison. The Commissioner consented, and our course began in April. So here we were, the experiment, prisoners learning their cultural heritage and history for the first time in our lives through a graduate student aligned to Phillips Brook House of Harvard University.

When I initially walked into the library I had noticed a stack of stapled, mimeographed, paper handouts sitting upon the table that was

27

serving as David's desk in the front of the room. Each handout appeared to be extremely thick, and kept drawing my attention and raising my curiosity. Once we had all settled into our seats, and pleasantries were exchanged between the tutor and his students, David suddenly asked us why we were all here. Some of us replied that we were here to learn our history. David shakes his head from side to side in a negatory response, and informs us that it is not the answer to the question he is asking. He then spreads his arms out to the side, in a gesture meant to signify the entire environment, and queries,

"Why are we here?", emphasizing with a nod of his head that he is talking about the prison.

Prisoner Henry Cribbs intones, "I'm here for murder."

Charles 2X McDonald, the only member of the Nation Of Islam present, says that he is in prison for allegedly violating the white man's laws.

Other, similar, answers are tossed into the discussion by the rest of us, and David patiently waits for the clamor to subside. He then looks around the room at our faces to insure that he has our undivided attention, and then points with the index finger of his right hand at the stack of mimeographed handouts neatly piled upon his makeshift desk.

"Directly, or indirectly," he says, "we are where we are today because of that."

Prisoner Ronald Penrose rises from his seat due to a nod from David, and passes out a copy of the handouts to each of us seated behind the tables. The handout reads: In the matter of Dred Scott versus John Sandford, and turns out to be the 254 page 1857 United States Supreme Court's decision. We spend the next 2½ sweat drenched hours reviewing the case law.

If I was not hot prior to reading the decision of the Court, I am a volcano now. Sweat pours from my brow onto the table...soaks my hands, and stains the papers I am holding, as I continue to read the opinions of the Justices regarding what they think of black people. David's assignment to us for the week is to finish reading the decision, and to be prepared to discuss what each of us believes the impact of the court's opinion has had upon our lives, and the lives of black people in this country as a whole.

I witness eleven unusually silent, yet angry, men leave the prison library this evening. I AM the twelfth angry man.

Back in my cell, in cellblock A3, as is my usual routine, I engage in my ritual of reading a poem before going to sleep. Tonight my routine is especially important, because my mind is reeling from having ingested U.S. Supreme Court Justice Roger B. Taney's decision of the court in the matter of Dred Scott. I am in need of a mental distraction. I choose a 1966 poem written by poetess Sonia Sanchez, entitled: "Blues." As my weary eyes begin to droop closed, I can hear Sonia whispering in my mind:

"in the night
in my half hour
negro dreams
I hear voices knocking at the door
I see walls dripping screams up
and down the halls..."

Enter the subtle metaphysics of the dream world: history superimposed upon the waking world to create a conscious dreaming body, as a vehicle to higher consciousness. Once the dream energies are fully awakened, unbound conscious perception comes alive. And here I am...standing upon the deck of a trireme ship...no sails...dead stop in front of a buoyed sign post whose inscription I cannot read, nor understand. There is nothing else around me, except barren space. The air is stale and stilled, yet agonized moans are reaching up to me from below deck, amidst the distinct rattle of chains. I have to move...have to run...but I cannot make a choice. Where should I go? Where can I go? I wring my hands, and in a cynical tone my hands speak to me:

"So here we have the negro rehabilitated...standing at the helm, governing the world with his intuition, rediscovered, reappropriated, in demand, accepted."

I begin to cry, because intuitively I recognize the voice of my hands to be that of the late Algerian social psychologist/revolutionary/author Frantz Fanon. He speaks to me through his open book, *Black Skin, White Mask*, like no other individual or author that I have encountered during my young life, and my hands and he are one singular voice:

"It is not a negro, oh no, but the negro, alerting the prolific antennae of the world, standing in the spotlight of the world, spraying the world with his poetic power, porous to every breath in the world."

My dream changes scenes during the course of the dialogue, to where I am no longer at the ship's helm. The sign post is gone. I haven't made a decision. Yet, here I am alone…cast in a spotlight, but still surrounded by darkness.

"I EMBRACE THE WORLD! I AM THE WORLD!", I scream into the nothingness of my dream stage, in the voice of Fanon.

The spotlight dims, and the stage becomes a replica of my childhood home in Lynn, Massachusetts. I am ten years old, in my second floor bedroom, having encased myself within an empty cardboard washing machine box that serves as my protection from the world…my fortress. I try to get out, but I cannot, as the box evolves into a steel barred cage surrounded by khaki uniformed white State prison guards. I am 21 years old again. Apparent to me, my guards are confused. They cannot understand the magical substitution of: slave to helmsman, cardboard to cage…man to child to man. But, Fanon has taught me that their are entrees that can only be served with my sauce!

As a magician, I stole away from my enslavement a certain world known only to myself and those like me—a world lost to my captors and their kind. When they realized that magic was in play, I believe that they must have felt an aftershock…something that they could not put their finger on and identify…unfamiliar to my reaction to their supremacist attitudes. The magic was that above their objective world of plantations, ghettoes, and prisons, I had subtly affirmed the real world. The essence of the real, natural, world was mine.

Frantz had succeeded in teaching me that between the real world and myself there is a relationship of coexistence, where I discovered the Primordial One. My speaking hands began to tear at the hysterical throat of their objective world. My captors realized that I was slipping away from their influence, and taking something of value with me. They began to search my pockets. They probed my very ideas and convictions, but came to the realization that there was nothing new. So, they thought, that I must be harboring a secret. They interrogated me, and not satisfied with my answers, they decided to systematically torture me in the form of Mississippi mistreatment.

I hear the voice of Billy Holiday singing "Strange Fruit" born of the "Liberty Tree," whose afterbirth is the steaming entrails of Mother Afrika being consumed by Ezekiel's horned beast. I am attached to the thickest limb of their oak tree by my right ankle…upside down…gelded, with my blood flowing into the gaping wound of my mouth…my left leg is bent at the knee into the shape of a figure four, as I am reformed to exemplify a card found in the tarot deck of Aleister Crowley's "Golden Dawn" ceremonial magicians. Symbolically and traditionally I am disfigured into the proverbial "Hanged Man." I turn away from my tormentors, and fade to black with an impervious air of mystery.

Here we are, my eleven classmates and myself, as children of ten playing the world…powerless…defenseless…besieged and disenfranchised, lost within the intestinal tract of the beast. Ahead of us, at the end of an exceptionally long segment of bowel, appears a golden light. We cautiously venture toward it, continuously slipping upon the bile covered tract. I feel drawn, as if by instinct. Within the light there appears the countenance of familiar black poets, bards, musicians, and historians…scholars. I recognize the voice of poetess Nikki Giovanni—a voice impressed upon my consciousness by her recording *Ego Tripping*; and in her soft melodic voice she recites from "Poem For Black Boys" to us:

"where are your heroes, my little ones
you are the Indian you so disdainfully shoot
not the big bad sheriff on his faggoty white horse
you should play run away slave
or mau mau
these are more in line with your history,"

as the annals of Black History that David Dance has taught me begin to unfold around me. Nikki continues,

"and you will understand all too soon
that you, my children of battle, are your heroes
you must invent your own games and teach us old ones
how to play."

My playmates dissolve, one by one. But, unlike the others, I never immerge from the bowels of the digesting beast. And, within this illusory/time-consuming environ, I see my own reflection cast upon the bile-coated membrane walls, and realize that I am now assembled within the ranks of the "old ones" that Nikki spoke of. A prisoner of my understanding and convictions, waiting to be taught the newest game to play by the children of the dream.

CHAPTER IV

ESSAYS:

SOCIETY—CULTURE—RACISM

THE SOCIALIZATION PROCESS OF
RALPH C. HAMM III

Race

The fact that I am ethnically of African origin, and descended from slaves, has a profound impact upon how I am viewed, both socially and politically, in American society. My earliest recollection of race occurred when I was eight years old. My father took me to my first baseball game at Fenway Park in 1959, where the white spectators and fans threw refuse (i.e., popcorn, beer, empty cups) and spit at us, while yelling racial epithets. I realized then that I was truly different, and not accepted in the company of whites because of my skin color...my race.

As I grew into my teens, and truly began to feel the brunt of de facto segregation, I came to understand that there were two separate sets of laws...two separate rules of etiquette...and two separate frames of reference in American society—one was white and the other was black. I came to look upon white people as the "other": those who look at the world through rose-tinted glasses, with a Disneyland (fantasy) concept of reality. I began to believe that they (white people) were my natural enemy, and not to believe a word that they said about anything. This belief was manifested in the 1960s, as one black leader after another... one civil rights worker after another...was murdered by members of white citizen groups, COINTELPRO, and/or local law enforcement. These witnessed murders were justified by the news media, on most occasions.

Consequently, growing up black in the 1950s-70s in America created within me a deep, burning, hatred for white America and everything labeled American. Fortunately for me, the 1970s was also the decade of enlightenment and Black Consciousness, as the movement spilled over from the 1960s. As I interpreted the movement, "Black Consciousness" was not inclusive to black people. It became my means of developing an awareness of where I fit in the culture of the world. The movement was significant to me because it was during the decade of the 1970s that I began to study African/African American history. As a consequence, I was empowered and influenced to study various ethnic histories other than my own. This study, course of, had the profound effect of transforming my bitterness and hatred into an overwhelming compassion for all human beings in general, and generated an empathy with other oppressed cultures and people. It was during this time period that I came to realize the oppressor in myself, come to terms with it, and come to understand the oppressor of materialism. I also learned that there was a biological basis for skin color, and that race differences have been utilized by colonists and imperialists throughout recorded history to divide, conquer, and enslave the masses of humanity.

Race is a social fiction, used by those who hold social and economic power, for the purpose of division and conquest.

Class

I believe that I initially became aware of class in the 1960s, when my working parents decided to move the family from Roxbury to Lynn, Massachusetts. I was 9 years old. Their openly debated reasons revolved around the fact that blacks from "down south" were moving into the housing projects where we lived, white families were moving out, and my parents were seeking upward mobility through the social stratum for their children. They did not want their children growing up in Roxbury with the non-working poor.

I gained a better understanding of class at the age of 22, when I began my studies in Black History and sociology. I became interested in class struggles and political science. I was not equating environmental variables (i.e., the concentration of factories and low-skilled labor, communications, mechanization) before 1973, when I began to distinguish class and the Walpole Prison population.

Today, I look at class through the lens of caste—Weber: writing that it is synonymous with ethnic status, honor, stratification with commercial classes, and the market.

Gender

Gender awareness began for me at the age of 4 or 5, when I became conscious of the fact that I was living in a family where six other individuals (my mother and five sisters) were different in physical appearance from my father and myself. Initially, I witnessed that my father went to work and provided for the family, while my mother stayed at home and looked after my sisters and myself.

This working arrangement changed in the 1960s, however, as the economy of the country began to shift and my mother was forced out of economic necessity to seek employment outside of the home. My siblings and I were delegated to perform the household chores in our mother's stead. Gender was no longer an issue as far as work was concerned, as I (the only male child) at times washed clothes, ironed, cleaned up after myself, made my own bed, and cooked for myself. So, it is safe for me to say that gender was first introduced to me by my parents as a division of labor, roles soon to be blurred by economics.

Sexuality

Sex and sexuality evolved with the onslaught of puberty...obtaining erections for no apparent reason at the age of 12, and seeking advice from my peers as to why this was happening to me, because my father had divorced my mother and the family at this period in my life. It was a confusing time for me.

By the time that I turned 14 I looked upon girls as sex objects to be desired and conquered through my wit, style, and my ability to take them out to the movies, dancing, or to the pizza shop. Every male in my peer group during this phase of my adolescence had to have a girlfriend, or he was regarded as less of a man...a sissy.

These concepts on sexuality took a dramatic turn when a friend in the Weather Underground sent me a book while I was imprisoned within Walpole State Prison entitled: *The Mass Psychology Of Fascism*, written by Wilhelm Reich. The book changed my perspective on sexuality, politics, religion, and society forever; to where I considered all facets of everyday life somehow controlled by the government and organized religion, as the means of sexual, psychological, and economic manipulation. Reich postulated that if an entity (religion or government) could control the human being's greatest impulse (to reproduce, or sex drive) through manipulation and fear, then that entity can control the human being for greater exploitation.

Religion

Religion in my family was big when I was a child. I was baptized in the Ruggle Street Baptist Church in Roxbury when I was 4 or 5 years old. I remember having to attend church and Sunday school every week with my older sisters. I also recall the fear and dread within me, whenever I sat in the congregation under the church's huge stained glass windows. I was afraid of God, not in love with him.

Organized religion taught me fear...to fear the unknown.

Today, after decades of studying the history of world religions, I no longer fear...I no longer accept the tenets of organized religion as universal truth. I transcended the need to seek God outside of myself, for in reality man is unified with all God is within himself. To the degree that he is conscious of that unification will he be able to express the Divine and demonstrate the power and perfection of the Divine in his body and in his affairs. All that there is of the individual—his body, mind, and spirit—is Divine.

Education

My earliest recollection of education occurred in 1955, when I was 4 years old. My two older sisters taught me how to read and write, much to the great surprise of my mother. The following year, at age five, I attended the Ira Allen Elementary School in Roxbury to begin kindergarten, and start the formal education process as a prospective member of American society.

Before attending public school, both of my parents instilled within us children that, as blacks, we had to study twice as hard and score twice as high on tests to achieve the grades reserved for our white classmates. Education for black children and adults was a necessity in Massachusetts if we, as a people, desired to vote. From a time before my parents' births, up until the Voters Rights Act of 1970 outlawed the practice, the Commonwealth enforced literacy tests to reduce the electoral participation of African Americans residing within the State—an adherence to the creed, and pathosis, of their Jim Crow heritage.

Public education is touted to be the initial state-sponsored orientation that a child receives in the process of becoming a productive citizen. However, public school education was for me a source of alienation and separation from the mainstream culture and society. My attendance in public schools throughout the 1950s-60s was a demeaning and degrading experience. I was taught that everything European, or white, was considered "good" and of importance, while everything of color (especially black) was to be considered evil and insignificant.

Public school attempted to reinforce within me the belief that Europeans (white people) were the only contributors to the storehouse of accumulated world achievement and knowledge. According to my public school education, Africa and Africans contributed nothing, with the exception of supplying America with satisfactory cotton pickers and cane cutters....maids and servants.

In the early 1970s, while incarcerated within the walls of Walpole State Prison, I was fortunate to have read *The Pedagogy Of The Oppressed* and *Education For Critical Consciousness* by Paolo Friere; as well as *Black Skin, White Mask* by Frantz Fanon. These two authors, in particular, altered my conception of education from a demeaning tool of repression and dominance to being the method toward mass liberation. I came to test their theories on education in 1973, while serving as an elected official in the National Prisoners' Reform Association, and they were correct. I have been in the struggle for my own liberation of consciousness through education ever since completing the reading of those books.

Books

I usually seek out literature on the subjects of: political science, liberation poetry, social history, social psychology, indigenous cultures, and world religious beliefs. The books that I choose to read have relevancy in my desire to know, and write books, based upon my experiences and a rounded view of the background and principles underlying the institutions that shape American life and impact upon society's beliefs. I continue to work upon my character and understanding, with books being the principle means through which to effect my evolution; given the environment in which I reside.

Sexism

This is the most difficult topic for me to discuss because, although I was raised by women (my mother and five sisters) and formally educated by women (teachers), I believe that I harbor sexist tendencies. I constantly catch, and reprimand, myself when I find that I am sexualizing and objectifying women on television...in movies...and even in the prison visiting room.

I try to convince myself that my behavior is due to having spent the past 46 years of my life in prison. There is the possibility that a portion of my sexist views come as a result of the predominately male prison environment where I have spent all of my adult life, as well as the result of the sensory intake of views reflected in the mainstream media and sub cultures of this country. I have no concrete answers, as there should be no excuses for my occasional behavior. All that can be honestly said is that I am aware of the problem, and that I am trying to address it.

I believe that I first became aware of the concept of sexism and gender bias while I was in elementary school. I was 5 or 6 years old. It happened during recess when the boys and girls were separated to play games—the boys played dodge ball, and the girls jumped rope or played hopscotch. It was forbidden for either gender to cross over to the others sport. Any boy who wanted to jump rope or play hopscotch was ridiculed and called a "sissy," and the girl who wanted to play dodge ball was held up to be a "tomboy." The boys accepted the "tomboys" amongst us, but not the "sissies"; although at this age no one knew what either term meant.

Homophobia

I cannot recall ever being afraid of homosexuals. The topic was not discussed at home, nor amongst my peers, so I had no adverse frame of reference. I first became aware of homosexuals while I was interred within the Essex County Training School at the age of 12. It was an all male facility that housed boys between the ages of 8 to 16. I never indulged the homosexuals there, but I did not blatantly avoid them because of their sexual preference either.

Upon leaving the Training School in 1966, I made a friend whose cousin was a transsexual. The cousin would dress and act feminine during the week and at work, but on the weekend he boxed to earn extra money at the Lowell Sun Arena in Lowell, Massachusetts. He always won the fights that I witnessed, and taught my friend and myself boxing skills; yet never made any sexual advances toward us. I liked him as a person, and my friend and I would often accompany him to shop for men's clothing when he wanted opinion into the latest fashion trends.

When I came to prison in 1969 I met more homosexuals, and I treated them the same way as I had treated my friend's cousin. Whatever was their sexual orientation was their life choice, not mine.

Family

My first recollection of the concept of family had to have occurred when I was around the age of three or four, or when I became cognizant of my environment. I knew my mother, father, sisters, and my grandmother and uncle on my father's side of the family. I knew that we were together, and my parents continually stressed how we were all family. With the exception of my grandmother and uncle, we all shared the same living space. We ate together, slept in the same dwelling, played games and went on outings together as a unit. Family to me, then, meant that I was never alone...that I was safe in their company...that I had nothing to be fearful about.

Today, family essentially means the same thing -- being cared about and cared for...that someone is watching out for my best welfare. The only distinction is that my extended family of friends and loved ones have proven to be more loyal and trustworthy than my immediate family.

HOW DO RACE AND
PUNISHMENT INTERSECT?

Beginning in colonial times in America, leaders and magistrates in the colonies meted out punishment to the settlers that were interpretations from the Bible. Most offenses were petty prior to the 18th century, and the crimes were primarily victimless.

Race and the severity of punishment made an appearance with the advent of perpetual slavery, wherein enslaved Africans held within the southern States fell victim to capital punishment more frequently than other ethnic groups. However, southern whites could also face capital punishment, especially if their crime was conspiracy with blacks to rebel against the conditions of chattel slavery. The main purpose of a more severe system of punishment appears then to have been premised upon an effort by plantation owners and the social elite to control slave rebellions, or the collaboration of the enslaved with whites and other free men. Southern plantation States often maintained a slave population that substantially outnumbered white settlers and property owners, therefore these southerners feared being overrun.

The Emancipation Proclamation of President Abraham Lincoln in 1863 ushered in an era of Reconstruction in the south, with the helpful addition of the 13th, the 14th, and the 15th Amendments to the United States Constitution. Michelle Alexander, in her book The New Jim Crow, rightfully contends that the 13th Amendment may have "abolished" slavery as a private institution, but the Amendment held the glaring exception of slavery being a proper "punishment" for those duly convicted of a crime (31). Southern legislators used the exception language of the 13th Amendment as their means to enact post-Civil War "Black Codes" and "Jim Crow Laws" whereby ex-slaves could not only be arrested, but also duly convicted for the petty crimes of vagrancy and idleness. Once convicted, under the color of State law, blacks were penalized and sentenced to hard labor on a convict-farm via convict-leasing. The black prisoners often found themselves leased to the plantations of their former slave owners. Existence on these farms and plantations proved to be more punitive, and deadlier, than life under chattel slavery. This was so because the former slaves were no longer considered by the plantation and farm owners as valuable property, they were now surplus human beings that could be readily replaced without a profit loss. Federal courts were not wont to act on the behalf of re-enslaved blacks because they used focus shifting tactics to determine that the re-enslavement was the result of State criminal statutes, and the federal court had no jurisdiction to dismantle the system. The court's principle way of thinking carried on for 80 years, or until the enactment of the 1965 Civil Rights Act.

Post-Civil War Reconstruction was indeed short-lived. Democratic Party politicians in the south implemented a strategy of 'Redemption' to force voting ex-slaves in their jurisdictions to switch party allegiances, and to retake the authority the whites felt that they had lost in the Civil War. 'The Mississippi Plan' was devised and utilized as the formula of intimidation, murder, and unspeakable violence to suppress the black vote, and to usurp the mandates of the 14th and 15th Amendments of the U.S. Constitution; assisted via acts of terror and murder carried out by such racist groups as the Redeemers and the Ku Klu Klan (formerly known as the Knight of the Golden Circle). The "Plan" was also instrumental in dissolving political coalitions between southern black and white Republicans.

Race has historically been utilized by white politicians as the means to drive wedges between poor blacks and whites who have formed socio-political coalitions. Race-based laws, with their ensuing punishments, have been implemented to bribe poor lower-class whites into breaking allegiances with blacks, and then to join political forces with the oppressor-elite for elusive social gains and status.

The twenty year span between the 1970s and the 1990s gave witness to white politicians aligning themselves with the news media, via the "war on crime" and "war on drugs" rhetoric designed to create and enact draconian race-based legislation (e.g., the crack cocaine laws), to expand the criminal-class as being black in America. These methods have manifested a new form of 'Redemption' in this country, as an effort to undermine the perceived political and socio-economic gains made by racial minorities during the late 1960s Civil Rights Era. According to Michelle Alexander, President Bill Clinton was a tremendous influence in perpetuating America's "current racial under caste," which was facilitated by his "tough on crime policies" and the dismantling of social welfare program safety nets (55-56). Clinton's policies have led to unprecedented numbers of black males incarcerated. Under the former President's direction, the expansion of punitive eviction policies utilized by the Department of Housing and Urban Development have produced expulsions from public housing, which has created an ever-increasing horde of homeless people in this country. The ruthless attacks by politicians upon the social welfare of urban America has incarcerated more citizens of color than in the history of the United States; and has socially, economically, and politically marginalized blacks to a limited space in society not unlike "Jim Crow."

THE CULTURE OF POVERTY

In his 1963 article "The Culture of Poverty," Oscar Lewis put forward that poverty is not visited upon all poor people, but finds itself residing within the psyche of those who "have a strong feeling of marginality, of helplessness, of dependency, of not belonging" (Lewis, 7). He further states that the poverty stricken are not people who think of themselves as such, but are unfortunates who are sensitive to their "status" in society. Such a culture has many facets.

Elijah Anderson informs us that black culture is an "oppositional culture" that has developed in direct response to the ideology of "alienation" (Anderson, 107). Reasons such as race, prejudice, and the systematic exclusion of black people from mainstream society, have been postulated by W.E.B. Dubois as being "all in the context of white supremacy" (Anderson, 108). The concept of white supremacy has marginalized black people through acts of discrimination, segregation, and sometimes terror. A drastic economic situation has occurred in which an "underground economy" of drug trafficking, prostitution, robbery, violence, and welfare scamming has emerged in the inner-city (spilling over to lower middle-class suburbia) to make up for the socioeconomic and legal restrictions that bar poor folks from access to the mainstream economy (Anderson, 109).

Another culture is the street culture in America, which is an offshoot of black culture, and in opposition to white culture. As a result of globalization, and deindustrialization, a plague of joblessness has engulfed the black community (in particular) and young men cannot find lucrative job opportunities. Thus, the illegal drug trade emerged as "the most lucrative and most accessible" means of economic gain (Lewis, 111). In direct response to the lack of trust in mainstream institutions, white people, and even middle-class blacks who have bought into America's economic system, young inner-city blacks have decided to actively live their lives in direct opposition to the mainstream by creating their own underground economies. Due to lack of faith in the justice system, black parents have instructed their children to "stand up for themselves physically or to meet violence with violence" (Anderson, 109), making them fodder for the criminal justice system and commodity-shares for the prison industrial complex.

The underground economy of drug trafficking brought with it a litany of peripheral social problems—violence, death, and the mass imprisonment of black males. "Crack culture" arose as "a reflection of the dislocations" in the black community, brought about by the transformation in the mainstream economy (Lewis, 120). The music, garment, jewelry, and automotive industry have all made a substantial monetary profit out of the inner-city drug culture (Lewis, 111-112), at the expense of the morality and mortality of the black community because the youth place more value on materialism than they do on spiritualism—in opposite to the values held by generations of inner-city predecessors.

As with most counter-cultures, unforeseen side effects have materialized as a result of fictive kinship affirmations. The need for self identity amongst black children of school age has hindered their pursuit of academic achievement, as the eurocentric educational curriculums have lent to demean any black historical contributions to world science and knowledge. The pursuit of education and academic success has been termed as "acting white," and has become a euphemism of degradation utilized by members of the inner-city poor who have accepted their position in the culture of poverty as being indelible and insurmountable, to belittle and stigmatize young students who are attempting to extract themselves from the culture through education (Fordham and Ogbu, 200-01). Without direct community intervention, and acknowledgement by the adults of the adverse effects of the above mentioned counter-culture influences upon impoverished children, black people will continue to marginally subsist like the proverbial crabs in a socio-economic barrel that is the culture of poverty.

References

Oscar Lewis. 1963. "The Culture of Poverty," reprinted in *Society* 35:7-9 (1998).

Elijah Anderson. 1999. *Code of the Street: Decency, Violence, and the Moral Life of the Inner City*. (New York: Norton); pages 106-141.

Signithia Fordham and John U. Ogbu. 1986. "Black Students' School Success: Coping With the 'Burden of Acting White,'" *Urban Review* 18:176-206.

CAUSES AND DISADVANTAGES OF
LOW-SKILLED URBAN WORKERS

The economic, political, and social disadvantages that inner-city residents often find themselves born into have forced them to adapt "norms" and "behaviors" that fall outside of those traditionally valued by mainstream American society, and thereby produce modes that form what Kenneth B. Clark describes as a "self perpetuating pathology." The symptoms of this pathology, according to Clark, include: poor education, low aspirations, drug addiction, alcoholism, unemployment, crime, family instability, and early death (Wilson, 4).

William Julius Wilson postulated that liberal social scientists have linked disadvantage to the problems experienced within the broader society, and have based their theories upon discrimination and "social class subordination" (5). Conservatives offer a different view, founded upon a theory that social welfare programs and government assistance have created a culture of dependency and "lack of initiative" (Wilson, 5). The mid 1960s through the 1980s witnessed liberals and conservatives contested in a war of words or definitions, in an effort to be the party to describe the plight of inner-city residents. The posturing gave ground to the conservative notion that ghetto dwellers lacked the initiative to pull themselves up and out of poverty, because they had become lazy and complacent from the government handouts.

Several factors lend themselves to the cause of socio-economic disadvantage that the low-skilled urbanite confronts. The shift in the economy from one of "manufacturing" (Danzinger and Gottschalk, 137), to a consumer-orientated economy produced the crippling effects of "globalization" (138). Low-skilled manufacturing jobs being outsourced to foreign union free markets abroad also contributed to large scale unemployment in the inner-city. Educational disadvantage, high technological and low tech sources of employment—"displaced by automation or had to compete with new imports" (149)—left the remaining employment opportunities in suburban areas, and thereby out of reach of the low-skilled inner-city work forces, according to Danzinger and Gottschalk. The middle class who had heretofore resided in black urban neighborhoods relocated to the suburbs in search of employment. A social drought evolved within black inner-city areas where the social, educational, and political institutions once supported by the working middle class became bankrupt due to the migration. Also, an example of a strong work ethic was lost to suburbia.

David K. Shipler adds another prism through which to view the plight of the disadvantaged, which resides within the workplace itself. For most low-skilled black workers, the place of suburban employment looms as a hostile environment and creates a "smothering sense of worthlessness" (129). This lack of self worth finds its roots in centuries of chattel slavery and the subsequent apartheid that is the political practice of marginalization of the urban poor by mainstream society and its institutions, passed on from generation to generation (132). The feeling of self-worthlessness becomes a self-fulfilling prophecy of low expectation, and a lack of initiative to enter mainstream society's working environment.

"The structural organization of society also plays a profound role in shaping the life chances of individuals" (Massey and Denton, 149). Segregation creates formidable barriers against economic and social aspirations, and curtails mobility. Without the ability to cross social barriers, low-skilled urban workers lack the vehicle through which to achieve economic gratification. The lack of education, technical skills, and employment contacts that were once available before the exodus of the black working class from the inner-city in pursuit of employment in suburbia, have made it difficult to overcome the disadvantage. Fluid mobility through the caste stratums of society imposed upon the urban poor due to their skin color, has left the black low-skilled potential urban workforce restricted to their dark corner of "dislocation" (Wilson, 3); as "spatial isolation leads to social isolation" (Massey and Denton, 161), leads to economic destitution.

References

Kenneth B. Clark, 1964., *Youth in the Ghetto: A Study of the Consequences of Powerlessness and a Blueprint for Change*, Harlem Youth Opportunities (HARYOU) Report.

William Julius Wilson, 1987. *The Truly Disadvantaged: The Inner City, The Underclass and Public Policy*. Chicago: University of Chicago. Chapters 1 and 2.

Sheldon Danziger and Peter Gottschalk, 1995. *America Unequal*. New York: Harvard University Press, Russell Sage Foundation. Chapters 7 and 8.

Douglas Massey and Nancy Denton, 1993. *American Apartheid: Segregation and the Making of the Underclass*. Chicago: University of Chicago Press. Chapter 6.

David K. Shipler, 2004. *The Working Poor: Invisible in America*. New York: Alfred A. Knopf. Chapter 5.

AN ARGUMENT FOR SUPPLEMENTAL
AFRICAN-CENTERED EDUCATION

Introduction

Historically, urban school children have been trapped within a public education system that has been designed to fail. Traditionally, those educators, politicos, and social engineers who are responsible for creating the environment of abject failure are entrusted with the grants and financial resources to find a remedial solution. Public school education claims to be the initial state-sponsored orientation that a child receives in the process of becoming a productive law-abiding citizen. If this is truly the case, then it is no wonder that the inner-city in particular, and America in general, are in severe trouble.

Many American educators and social engineers are in the habit of blaming the victims, black families and their children, for the crisis confronting the public school system. The blame is cast about as if inner-city children have the wherewithal and intellectual capacity to educate themselves. Daniel Patrick Moynihan warned that "Low education levels in turn produce low income levels, which deprive children of many opportunities, and so the cycle repeats itself" (Moynihan, 31). It is obvious that the cycle Moynihan spoke of must be broken.

The most overlooked inter-connection between Africans and Europeans that has been negated, discarded, or minimized, is chattel slavery. The African holocaust is rarely, if ever, fully explained or taught in public school. The relationship between the white slave trader and the enslaved African are ties that have bound us together for centuries.

"Negroes in bondage, stripped of their African heritage, were placed in a completely dependent role. All their rewards came not from individual initiative and enterprise, but from absolute obedience—a situation that severely depresses the need for achievement among all people" (Moynihan, 19-20).

Signithia Fordham and John Ogbu concluded that black children do not perform well in public school because of [1] the "inferior" quality of education and ill-treatment they receives while they are in school, [2] whites have imposed a "job ceiling" and then do not adequately reward black children for their academic achievements later on in life, and [3] blacks develop "coping devices" and counter-cultures that hinder their ability to pursue success in academia (Fordham and Ogbu, 179). Curriculums taught in public school seldom portray blacks and other ethnic minority groups in a positive image, and instead emphasize contributions, achievements, heritage, and cultures of Europe and white America. Public school, thereby, fosters resentment, alienation, and feelings of inferiority among black school children. But, there is a solution.

Methodology

I suggest that only through a supplemental education of African-American heritage and history can the true reversal begin of what Dr. Joy Degruy Leary describes as "Post Traumatic Slave Syndrome."[1] African-American children will be afforded a viable opportunity to achieve self-worth and self-sufficiency through a program designed with both supplemental education and vocational training components, as the means to endeavor to strive for their full academic and social potential.

African-American children require an African-centered pedagogy because world-wide Eurocentric hegemonic attitudes, educational systems, politics, and policies remain in effect to this day. As a result, the social and educational status of most African-Americans has not significantly changed, relative to whites, throughout the course of history in America. Becky Pettit argues that

"Black men have experienced no improvement in high school completion rates since the early 1990s, and significant racial inequality in educational attainment among men persists even five decades after Brown v. Board of Education. Such findings call into question the assumed egalitarian effects of the educational system." (Pettit, 68).

I concede that public school education can:

1. Instill superficial citizenship skills through a basic understanding of this country's political system—supported by promoting, questioning, and fundamental critical thinking skills;

2. Attempt to teach adequate literacy skills, mathematics,

humanities, and basic technologies that are required in order to negotiate economic self-sufficiency in mainstream society; and,

3. Provide a Eurocentric historical overview of America as an European melting pot, and the world, that represents predominantly Europe's ethnic contribution to the storehouse of accumulated knowledge.

My suggestion for an African-American supplemental education curriculum is designed to offer a specific pedagogical experience that reflects the following attributes necessary in cultural specificity:

1. Legitimize African stores of knowledge;
2. Legitimize and build upon the indigenous languages of the African continent;
3. Reinforce community ties, and idealize service to family, community, nation, ethnicity, and the world;
4. Promote positive social relationships;
5. Positively promote productive community and cultural practices;
6. Instill a social and political world view that idealizes a positive, self-sufficient, future for African-Americans without denying the self-worth and right to self-determination of others;
7. Support cultural continuity while simultaneously promoting critical consciousness; and,
8. Promote a spiritual ontological foundation (ex., kemetic cosmology) to build moral character.

Conclusion

The importance of African-centered supplemental education is necessary to foster ethical character, morality, and self-worth in black children. Public school education and the media have collaborated in contributing "to vacant esteems formation" within the minds of African-American children, as blacks are often portrayed as "academically deficient," which impacts upon a child's "assessment of their own worth," according to Dr. Leary (130-131).

African heritage and cultural character has a sociological ontology that remains consistent, and should be redeemed as a reconstruction of lost heritage. It is the foundation of an effort to reclaim the sense of self that was stripped away from Africans brought to America during the centuries of chattel slavery. A spiritual ontological foundation based upon African religions is important because the religious beliefs of the west cannot be trusted to instill ethics and morality in black youth, especially since "Christianity has long tolerated or made common cause with the terrorizers who build imperial regimes of oppression" (Mark Taylor, 70), as has been the history of America and its ill-treatment of African slaves and their descendants.

> "[In the United States] the slave was totally removed from the protection of organized society...his existence as a human being was given no recognition by any religious secular agency... completely cut off from his past, and he was offered absolutely no hope for the future" (Moyniham, 18)

If the children are indeed the future, then the United States appears to have a future that is bleak, and extremely forbidding as an outlook for African-American children attempting to make their way into mainstream society through the public education system.

Notes

1. "Post traumatic slave syndrome" is a condition that exists when a population has experienced multi-generational trauma resulting from centuries of slavery and continues to experience oppression and institutionalized racism today. *Post Traumatic Slave Syndrome: America's Legacy of Enduring Injury and Healing*; page 125.

References

Fordham, Signithia; Ogbu, John D., "Black Students' School Success with the 'Burden of Acting White'"; *Urban Review* 18: 176-206

Leary, Dr. Joy Degruy, *Post Traumatic Slave Syndrome: America's Enduring Legacy of Injury and Healing*, (Milwaukee Oregon: Uptone Press, 2005)

Moynihan, Daniel Patrick, *The Negro Family: The Case for National Action*, (Washington D.C.: Office of Policy Planning and Research, 1965)

Pettit, Becky, *Invisible Men: Mass Incarceration and the Myth of Black Progress*, (New York: Russel Sage Foundation, 2012)

JUST PREY TO THE GODS

As America is still reminded by the media to mourn 9/11, the children killed en masse in Colorado, Connecticut, and recently the April 15, 2013 Boston Marathon bombing (ushering in "Boston Strong"); political pundits, so-called news media experts and their ilk, have subsided in their clamor for stiffer gun control laws, public safety, capital punishment and longer prison terms, and greater homeland security (sacrificing more Constitutional protections, until there are none), until the next catastrophe arises.

Through the intentional use of fun house mirrors and smoke-screens, the general public in America appear to be stymied... dumbfounded...over how anyone (homegrown or otherwise) could or would unleash such horrific and violent acts against "soft targets" in this society, conveniently overlooking the fact that similar acts of horror and violence were perpetrated against native American women and children and are the cornerstone of the founding of this nation. There are innumerable deaths by gun violence within this country every year (Trayvon Martin yesterday, today...), with young black males carrying the heaviest of tolls—be that through gang/street violence, domestic violence, police/security violence or judiciary violence.

Author Tom Engelhardt so aptly stated:

"The Greeks had it right. When you live on Mount Olympus, your view of humanity is qualitatively different. The Greek gods, after all, lied to, stole from, lusted for, and punished humanity without mercy while taking the planet for a spin. And it didn't bother them a bit. They felt—so Greek mythology tells us— remarkably free to intervene from the heights in the affairs of whichever mortals caught their attention and, in the process, to do whatever took their fancy without thinking much about the nature of human lives. If they sometimes felt sympathy for the mortals whose lives they repeatedly threw into havoc, they were incapable of real empathy. Such is the nature of the world when your view is the Olympian one and what you see from the heights are so many barely distinguishable mammals scurrying about."[1]

Today's America is yesterday's Mount Olympus. The inner cities, native American reservations...The Iraqs, Afghanistans, Palestines, Pakistans, Egypts, Syrias, Rwandas, Darfurs of the world are "soft targets" for American sanctioned violence, guns, bombs, UAVS, and asundry weapons of mass destruction descending down from the heights upon thousands of human targets like Olympian gifts from the Mount (White House, State department, military industrial complex). But these have become acceptable targets of a differing hue, religion, language, culture, than mainstream America; and therefore, that much more acceptable as casualties (collateral damage) in the "War on Drugs" ..."War on Terror"..."War on Humanity." Mainstream America is not accustomed to being the prey in a war, and therefore cannot imagine what it means to exist under the gun day after day...year after year. The new Olympians have immunized their senses to the screams emanating from the inner cities of humanity for decades, as the means of conditioning themselves against the...world.

True suffering is only suffering when Mount Olympus suffers.[2]

As the minions and subjects of the children lost in the Colorados, Connecticuts, Bostons, and possibly Floridas of this country, bearing witness to the banners billowing at half-mast...the tiny coffins draped in funeral shrouds. Foreign dignitaries/allies send their condolences, heartfelt or as a matter of tribute to the Mount. But, as a country with god-like attitudes, do we mourn the other hundreds of babies of a different hue around the globe who have fallen victim to America's gun violence and worship? Yet, all of these human sacrifices to New Mount Olympus are someone's babies. It takes mass violence in a New Olympian suburban community to attract the nation's attention for a brief moment and solicit a pseudo-response. Then the weapons lobbies react, and shut down the half-hearted response to the epidemic of violence that has plagued inner city communities forever and has evolved into a virulent culture of death; while mothers of a different hue mourn their dead babies in relative obscurity.

Babies shoot and kill other babies, with the survivors often condemned to languish in prison plantations in New Olympus under the onus of life sentences, because they succumbed to the economy of the culture of violence through marginalization. These children are sentenced to life in prison by a judiciary manned by judges who wield the power of life and death—who depend upon the violence of mortals for their very existence (self-worth), making them the most violent of us all. As the perpetrators become the victims, we the subjects of Mount Olympus pay homage to our man-made gods, via one form of living currency or another.

The world has become the backyards, main streets, battle fields, prisons, and graveyards of the New Olympian Order.

Notes

1. *The United States of Fear*, Haymarket Books (Chicago: 2011), page 67.
2. We mortals must suffer through the violence perpetrated against us by the New Mount Olympus and their minions with humility, but we are forbidden to defend ourselves or fight back; nor can we protest too loudly, or an even more severe punishment will rain down upon us from on high.

CHAPTER V

ESSAYS:

POLITICS—JUSTICE SYSTEM

COMMONWEALTH VS. RALPH C. HAMM III:
A COMPELLING MATTER OF RACE

In 1968 I was a codefendant in a criminal episode when I was 17 years old and in the company of two adults who initiated an attack upon a young white couple in Lawrence, Massachusetts. I was sentenced to serve a controlling second degree life sentence for a violation of Massachusetts General Law, chapter 265, section 24—assault with intent to rape. All three codefendants are black, which the 1984 Massachusetts Appeals Court (upon my post conviction appeal) utilized as a determinant factor in ruling that my trial counsel (Bruce N. Sachar) gave me advice that was "reasonable and not the result of incompetence," when coercing me to waive trial by jury under the threat that the jury would be all white and unable to afford me a fair trial [Commonwealth v. Ralph C. Hamm, 471 Northeast 2d 416, 421]. The jury waiver was coerced by court-appointed trial counsel without Sachar ever first using voir dire or filing a motion for change of venue, nor a motion to discover the material/physical evidence in the criminal proceeding (example; forensic exculpatory evidence of blood type, fingerprints, and handprints testified to at trial by the police to have been found throughout the interior of the 1965 Ford Mustang fastback automobile, where the charged assault with intent to rape was testified to have occurred). My codefendant Robert Preston was stabbed above his eye by the knife wielding second codefendant Emanuel Smith, and was profusely bleeding over everything and everyone. I was never in the automobile. Nor did Bruce Sachar independently investigate any of the material facts offered at trial by the Commonwealth prior to trial, in violation of the Massachusetts Canon of Ethics, because he was in essence working as a co-prosecutor beside his long time friend Assistant District Attorney Peter Brady.

The 1984 Appeals Court ruled that Bruce Sachar, as trial attorney, did not have to independently investigate the material facts of the criminal case, because he "had access to the prosecutor's case file," [Id., at 421], and further, that Sachar's defense strategy was "of a legal and not factual nature" [Id., at 421]. In other words, all that Bruce Sadhar was required to do was to show a legal presence in the court room by sitting next, to me, to make the proceedings appear to be legitimate for the sake of conviction. By Sachar's ability to access the prosecutor's case file prior to trial, he knew that the Commonwealth was going to claim that the assault with intent to rape was to have occurred upon the backseat of the automobile, with me kneeling over the female victim. Yet, Sachar acquiesced Brady's release of the automobile back to the custody of the male victim two weeks before the trial (without ever seeing it) and never compared the Mustang's backseat area dimensions to Ralph's six foot six inch stature. Sachar also failed to adequately cross examine the victims (only 1½ pages of trial transcript), and testified at my 1980 motion for a new trial hearing that he determined the victims had "been through enough already."

By the time of my post conviction appeal in 1980, Bruce N. Sachar had become the president of the Essex County Bar Counsel, and no judge in Massachusetts was going to rule that he was ineffective during Ralph's trial. Sachar's political clout, and the protection afforded him by his peers, stands in the way of any fair review and determination in Commonwealth v. Ralph C. Hamm to this very day.

In 1972 Massachusetts General Law, chapter 265, section 24 was amended by the State legislature for being too Draconian in its severity of mandating a life sentence for intending to commit rape. However, I remain the only person in Massachusetts jurisprudence to be serving a life sentence under the old statute because, as the Massachusetts Appeals Court would determine in 1984 in upholding the Superior Court denial of his motion for a new trial in 1980, "Hamm is black and his victims white" [Id. at 421].

As a result of the racism inherent within the 1984 Appeals Court Decision, the Massachusetts Parole Board has interpreted it as a green light to modify my second degree life sentence with a 15 year parole eligibility date (Massachusetts General Law, chapter 127, section 133A) into a natural life sentence, by suggesting to me on three separate occasions during his 2009 parole eligibility hearing to die in prison because of my beliefs (convictions).

My two codefendants were released from Massachusetts prison custody over 20 years ago, after striking post-Conviction sentencing deals with the Essex County District Attorney's Office. Codefendant Emanuel Smith, the oldest of the criminal defendants who was the initiator of the attack in 1968, and the Commonwealth's chief prosecution witness during my 1969 trial, made a secret sentencing deal with the prosecution through his attorney to testify (lie) against me at his trial. My two codefendants are relatives, which left me as the odd man out. Smith was released from Massachusetts prison custody in 1984, and within ten years managed to become a codefendant with another of his relatives in Maryland, in a more heinous attack upon a white couple there, where he remains in prison.

To add insult to injury, the Sex Offender Registry Board (SORB) has determined that I was to be the only one of the three criminal defendants to be ranked as a level 3 sex offender, for my conviction of assault with intent to rape. This in the face of the fact that I am still imprisoned, the parole board has no intentions of affording me a parole, and I am still serving a life sentence where me codefendants are not in State custody. Also, the fact that the offense occurred in 1968 when I was 17 years old and in the company of two adult offenders, has no bearing upon my designated high level of risk as a juvenile at the time of the crime first offender.

In Massachusetts, adult multiple child rapists and repeat rapists often receive level 1 and level 2 by the SORB. Also, in the Commonwealth, a codefendant can aid the State in convicting a criminal defendant for a crime, but his testimony is suspect and will not be used to exonerate the same defendant; which is why it has become prudent for the prosecution (in league with the defense) to withhold, and/or to leave undiscovered, all exculpatory physical evidence from trial.

As the Massachusetts Appeals Court decided in 1984, any application of Constitutional protections during the procedural history of my conviction will always derive from the matter of race.

TO: The Yale Law Journal
Attn: Prison Law
P.O. Box 208215
New Haven, CT 06520-8215

FROM: Ralph C. Hamm III (#W32301)
Massachusetts Correctional Institution
P.O. Box 43
Norfolk, MA 02056

DATE: July 21, 2012

RE: PRISON LAW WRITING CONTEST

ESSAY: A BLACK MAN'S SOCIOLOGICAL ANALYSIS OF THE MASSACHUSETTS CRIMINAL JUSTICE SYSTEM AND DEPARTMENT OF CORRECTIONS

As a teenager, prior to my 1968 criminal activity and subsequent conviction in 1969, my view of the criminal justice system was considerably obscure...opaque. I suppose that I harbored an outlook that was similar to that of most people living in the United States who did not have an intimate experience with the machinations of the criminal justice process. My overview was textbook: (a.) I believed that the police never lied, (b.) the criminal justice system was just, (c.) judges were above reproach and did not discriminate, (d.) criminals received what they deserved, (e.) innocent people did not go to prison, and if so, (f.) the truth would immediately prevail and set them free. Conditions, norms and values, whereby the ends and means were selected.

Pathologist Observation of Criminal Justice System.

[DEFINITION: The study of the origin, nature, and course of any deviation from a healthy, normal, or efficient condition.]

Based upon my pathologist point of view of the criminal justice system at age seventeen, I believed that although I was guilty of specific

65

crimes against the male victim of my criminal episode, I would be vindicated by the trial process of any criminal involvement attached to the female victim for which I was innocent. Somewhere lodged within my adolescent mind were the lessons and impressions instilled from my junior high school civics classes, the news media, and a piece of paper entitled the Constitution of the United States of America—where all men were innocent until proven guilty…everyone had a right to a jury of their own peers…one had the right to effective assistance of trial counsel…all men were created equal. I was naive. For, what if one was considered subhuman? What if one's ancestors were considered as property to the so-called founding fathers, and regarded as only three-fifths of a human being, at the signing of the Constitution? What would be the safeguards utilized at trial to preserve Constitutional rights, and to determine the final outcome then?

In 1969 I came to learn that the criminal justice system in Massachusetts was not founded upon the truth, nor was it color blind (as I had been led to believe); rather, it was based upon who could tell the most convincing lie—especially if that lie was against a black person.

My perception of the criminal justice system was further altered in the 1970s, when I read the 1857 United States Supreme Court decision In The Matter Of Dred Scott versus John Sandford, in conjunction with Ralph Ellison's novel *Invisible Man*. I came away from these readings with an awakened consciousness and a point of view that the black man in America had no civil nor human rights that white people in this country were bound by law to respect. If, therefore, I was seeking justice for a perception of Constitutionally-based wrongs perpetrated against me, then I had better generate my own light source. This was so because my sense of self and worth were not visible to the white man's eye. I still viewed the system as a pathologist, but now it had become someone else's fault for my imprisonment and not the result of my actions.

Presently, I view the criminal justice system through a much clearer lens. I have come to realize that some of my prior notions that found root within my pathologist phase still held true, but they have been tempered by education, experience, and time…detached from most of my personal biases, and grounded in evidence. I look more to the 'actions' of human beings within the criminal justice system, and to their conflicting theories of how the system is supposed to function. I have come to realize that it is less about me, specifically, than it is about maintaining a well-oiled and overtly racist tool for social control of the marginalized poor in this country. There is nothing about true crime prevention and control inherent within the system.

As my years in prison advanced into decades, I witnessed Massachusetts' racial minority communities implode upon themselves due to the systematic economical and social disenfranchisement associated with the globalization of the workforce, as well as the stigma associated with prison. I have witnessed the sons of fellow and ex prisoners follow in their fathers' footsteps through the criminal justice system—entering the prison system with young children in their wake, just like their fathers before them, and leaving the children to be raised by young black mothers. They enter the criminal justice system with little or no formal education or vocational skills—functionally illiterate—and often leave through the prison doors back to society in the same manner. The absenteeism of the father role model throws the family out of balance, leaving adolescent boys (and often girls) to mature without a male adult in the family unit to pattern behavior. No male role model at home often results in the seeking of that male bonding in street/drug gangs, and the child's embracing a counter culture that utilizes criminal activity (i.e., drug selling, drug use, robbery, home invasions, violence against others) as a rite of passage into adulthood. These adopted rites often lead to the criminal justice system, and the Department of Corrections (DOC).

The road to the criminal justice system is paved with substandard education, social and economic marginalization, the outsourcing of lucrative employment opportunities overseas and out of the inner-city into suburban areas, destruction of the social welfare safety net, and the unceasing siege upon people of color by government agencies and their supportive institutions (i.e., educational, judicial, political, and media) via an illusory war on drugs and crime.[1]

Participant Observation of the Criminal Justice System

[DEFINITION: Participant observation refers to a close and intimate familiarity with a given area of study through an intensive involvement with people in their natural environment.]

Research vehicles: a). direct observation, b). self analysis, c). participation in the life, d). life history, e). discussions, and f). informal interviews.

—Police often beat and/or threaten at gunpoint (co)defendants upon their arrest.

RESULT: Coerced identification, and false confessions to crime.

—Lawyer(s) usually visits defendant once while awaiting trial, or only upon court dates, or does not visit with client at all prior to the trial.

RESULT: Softens up the defendant/client for plea bargaining, and psychologically impairs him to accept anything that the lawyer may suggest during the course of the trial.

—The lawyer withdraws as paid counsel prior to the trial in an effort to obtain a court-appointment as defense counsel.

RESULT: The court appointment insures that counsel works in the best interest of the Commonwealth and not in his client's best interest, to secure future court appointments from the State. It is impossible to serve two masters.

—The court appointed lawyer tells his client to waive his right to a trial by a jury, because the jury will be all white and the defendant will not receive a fair trial. The waiver is hand written by the attorney and hastily signed by the defendant, without any foreknowledge as to what the duties of a jury might entail.

RESULT: This subterfuge allows the trial to proceed without an independent twelve person fact-finder, and allows any exculpatory physical evidence to be withheld from the trial. Trial counsel is thereby excused from performing any pre-trial discovery into the material facts of the case or the State's evidence, and can thereby rely upon the prosecutor's case file in direct opposition to the Canon of Ethics (in essence, adopt the role of co-prosecutor).

—The court-appointed lawyer informs the defendant that codefendant(s) or material witnesses do not want to take the witness stand or cannot be found at trial.

RESULT: Material witnesses and exculpatory evidence is lost to the defense.

—A codefendant pleads guilty to lesser charges, and testifies for the Commonwealth during the trial of the defendant.

RESULT: Due to lack of discovery, the court does not know that the Commonwealth's witness has been coerced by the prosecutor and threatened by the arresting police, as well as offered a secret sentencing deal through his attorney to testify against the defendant.

—All forensic and exculpatory evidence is withheld from bench trial.

RESULT: The lack of a jury affords court-appointed counsel the excuse not to view the scene of the crime, not to ask for an independent test to be conducted upon finger and hand prints, blood, testified by the prosecution to have been found at the crime scene, nor to effectively cross examine the victims of the crime.

—Court-appointed counsel affords no closing argument at the conclusion of the trial, but instead concedes to the prosecution.

RESULT: Defense rests, and client is found guilty.

—Massachusetts Practice Rules Of Procedure, Rule 30, replaces the once statutorily mandated writ of habeas corpus in the State.

RESULT: Appellate Courts now make decisions on criminal cases via focus shifting away from central Constitutional arguments, as well as afford decisions that are short on law—where coerced jury waivers become counsel's advice to waive the jury (a true example of Orwellian "double speak"),[2] and thereby reasonable due to the skin color of the victims of crime and the criminal defendant; thus avoiding the claim of an unconstitutional jury waiver. Trial counsel's lack of pre-trial discovery , or independent investigation of the physical evidence and facts of the case, is justified based upon a claim of a legal and not factual defense strategy by trial counsel (i.e., physical evidence is determined irrelevant in the face of a legal supposition of guilt).[3]

Conclusion

If the criminal defendant is indigent, and cannot afford the tens of thousands of dollars required to hire competent defense counsel in Massachusetts, it can be expected that he will not receive even a modicum of fairness or due process at his trial. The systematic usurping of Constitutional protections will inevitably result in a finding of guilt. This outcome is especially egregious when the defendant is black and the alleged victim is white, most noticeably during the sentencing phase. If and when the defendant appeals his conviction through the post-conviction process when the victim is white, the Commonwealth advances the notion "in the interest of the Commonwealth" to the reviewing court, in support of the conviction. Constitutional arguments do not surmount the interest of the Commonwealth, because a black person is not considered as a part of the Commonwealth except in regard to being property...because the wealth referred to is not representative of the common man, whose interest does not actually matter; and the appeal fails.

Subjectivist Observation of Department of Corrections.

[DEFINITION: The doctrine that all knowledge is limited to experiences by the self, and that transcendent knowledge is impossible.]

I was sentenced to prison in June of 1969, and from the very first day of incarceration the Department of Corrections was for me "the system" (or, as Peter Tosh the reggae singer would say: "the shit-stem").

By way of my own self-induced form of regression therapy (prior to any knowledge of Sigmund Freud and his methodology), I systematically traced my short life experiences through childhood, family disillusionment, youth angst (delinquency), military service, criminal episode and trial, up to my present prison(er) predicament. I attempted to retrace my missteps honestly, in an effort not to fall victim of the multiple psychological weapons aimed at me by my prison environment.

I reached the conclusion that the DOC is nothing more (or less) than a monster factory—a perpetual slave manufacturing behemoth designed to piece together semblances of human beings (like Dr. Frankenstein's laboratory), and recycle them in and out through an assembly line to their factory outlets (i.e., the inner-city communities).

America, through (a). social marginalization of its lowest income citizenry, to (b). sub-standard institutions of elementary education whose tracking system encourages dropouts...abhorrent behavior...and rebellion against the social order, to the (c). juvenile justice apparatus, eventually to (d). adult criminality onto prison or the DOC; the cycle of control is maintained against people of color, generally, making them the commodities of the prison-industrial-complex (PIC).

I have witnessed the monster recycling process perpetuated against generation after generation of inner-city denizens for over four decades, during my imprisonment. When one speaks of the criminal justice/ DOC apparatus, one must accept parole[4] and probation as an integral part of the machine, as well as a principal recycling agency.

Participant Observation Analysis of the Department of Corrections.

—Inner-city public school failure is designed into the educational system to create surplus human beings (everyone cannot be allowed to graduate high school and attend college, for there would then be an overabundance of unemployed educated people—intelligent cause for rebellion)...lack of substantive employment opportunities for the under educated...social and economical segregation, away from partaking in mainstream societal benefits...enforced low self-esteem; have all contributed to creating a crime ridden drug/street gang under caste culture of inner-city youth.

RESULT: The DOC has become the chief warehousing agency to inter and store those adjudged to be surplus human beings, and therefore unfit to participate within mainstream society.

—The outsourcing of low paying, low skilled, jobs in the manufacturing industry has created a service-related economy.

RESULT: Departments of Corrections across the country have become the leading employer of the lower middle-class, and a quasi-law enforcement labor market.

—Media and politician induced hysteria over inner-city crime and punishment.

RESULT: Although the crime rate is down across the country, the DOC fulfills the psychological role of control over lower income minority group communities, their birth rates, curtailment of their voting efforts; and thereby physically contributes to maintaining the status quo.

—Limits self-awareness, self-responsibility, self-growth, and self-esteem.

RESULT: The DOC alienates its wards from society, from advances in technology, and serves to destroy family ties. It restricts educational and vocational training, similar to the mainstream, which would aid in making an individual self-sufficient. The DOC keeps its wards relatively functionally illiterate, as a method of system dependency and control.

—Maintains an in-house pecking order amongst prisoners and staff employees, pitting them against one another.

RESULT: The DOC, perpetuates America's societal caste system and racism, thereby preventing its victims from truly acknowledging the source of their suffering, despair, and exploitation.

—Its wards are fed an extremely high carbohydrate diet, and are sold high carbohydrate foodstuffs for exorbitant prices in the prison canteen/store.

RESULT: Sugar addiction. High incidences of diabetes, especially in the young who come from inner-city families that are relegated to sub exist off of high carbohydrate diets, creates a pharmaceutical dependency for life and an early mortality.

—DOC wards are forced to drink , and bathe in, water that is contaminated with human feces and other toxic substances.

RESULT: High incidences of skin infections, close to chronic diarrhea, and intestinal ailments. The staff of the prison facilities are afforded an annual multi-million dollar water allotment in their contract for safe drinking water; while the wards of the State are extorted to pay eighty cents for a sixteen ounce bottle of "Poland Springs" filtered water (if they are not indigent) from the prison canteen/store, where the same company sells twenty-four bottle cases of twenty-four ounce bottles of their water for six dollars in the outside community.

—Prohibits meaningful prisoner-run self-help programs to exist, and condones staff harassment of community volunteers and teachers.

RESULT: The DOC perpetuates the notion of dependency and well being of the slave upon the master, both materially and psychologically, to destroy any sense of self-reliance before releasing him back into the community.

—The DOC maintains its own abhorrent behavior modification and treatment programs, via State and federal grant money.

RESULT: DOC treatment programs are a farce, and a squandering of public funds. For example, the sex offender treatment program (SOTP) targets sex offenders with adult victims (the second lowest recidivist group to commit the same crime) for a reverse therapy program that coerces offenders to admit to prior fantasy offences or deviancies for the benefit of district attorneys for their civil commitment hearings (a multi-million dollar boondogle). The DOC, keeps statistics on this program to claim low recidivism as a result, when the statistics were already low for repeat sexual assaults upon adults, which have not changed dramatically prior to the 1997 inception of the program. The Corrections Recovery Academy (CRA) also lends the appearance of being an abject failure. As a self-proclaimed drug rehabilitation program, more of its prisoner clients fail urine sample drug testing, and are disciplined for drug use, than those prisoners with drug abuse in their record who do not attend the CRA, program. There resides the appearance that more prisoner graduates from the CRA, recidivate back to prison than those prisoners who did not attend. The DOC, has no accountability for the CRA, and has thus far refused to keep statistics on their success and failure rates. Both of the aforementioned programs afford a public delusion that the programs exist to promote effective public safety, when in truth they exist to generate State and Federal funding in an effort to create a greater DOC, operating budget and bureaucracy.

—The DOC, releases angry, unskilled, and disoriented surplus human beings back into the community via completion of sentence and parole.

RESULT: The department successfully creates the mechanism through which those released will have a greater chance of perpetrating more crimes, or violating their conditions of parole, and thereby be recycled[5] back into the prison-industrial-complex by society as a cash crop. The mechanism guarantees job security and momentum in the service-related economy.

—The Massachusetts Parole Board acts as a sister agency to the DOC, and the criminal justice apparatus of the State, in their joint effort to recycle surplus human beings as well as keep them interred as economic commodities. Recently, the United States Supreme Court decided in

Miller v. Alabama (No. 10-9646. Argued March 20, 2012—Decided June 25, 2012) that juvenile offenders under the age of eighteen can no longer be sentenced to life imprisonment without the possibility of parole for homicide; citing Graham v. Florida, 560 U.S._____(2010), which held that juveniles could no longer be sentenced to life in prison without the possibility of parole for non-capital offenses.

RESULT: The criminal justice apparatus of the State has zeroed in on the language "possibility of parole" held within both U.S. Supreme Court Decisions as the vehicle to amend natural life sentences for juveniles to parole eligible second degree life sentences (pursuant to Massachusetts General Law, chapter 127, section 133A) that contain a fifteen year parole eligibility date. In Massachusetts, the parole board is manned by ex county prosecutors and former members of law enforcement who, in their vindictiveness and through their broad discretionary power as board members, will obviously repeatedly deny parole to juvenile offenders who have had their natural life sentences converted to second degree life sentences, and impose five year parole eligibility reviews ad infinitum; thereby insuring that the juvenile offender continues to serve a natural life sentence and dies in prison as a result of the continued parole set backs.[6]

—UMASS Medical, the health care provider that is contracted by the Department of Corrections, has the green light to extort extra medical fees from prisoners outside of their contract stipulation and State law.

RESULT: Prisoners are deprived of necessary dentures to masticate their food properly, after years of having their real teeth extracted by DOC, contracted dentists, unless they additionally pay $32-$169 lab fees on top of the $3 co-pay established by law; while male prisoners who desire sex changes, to grow breasts and have their penis surgically converted into a vagina, can obtain the procedure free of charge with no lab fees attached. The lack of dentures creates painful sores in the mouth, gum disease, acid reflux disease, esophagus and gastrointestinal problems, and possible stomach cancer (exasperated by the ingestion of polluted water from prison sinks); which are 8th Amendment violations of cruel and unusual punishment. The cost of one sex change and after treatment would probably pay for thousands of sets of dentures for needy prisoners.

Conclusion

The DOC is utterly repressive, punitive, and vindictive by design and purpose. The general public is led to believe that a person is in prison to pay for their crime against society, and will not be released therefrom without first being remorseful for the wrongdoing and showing signs of rehabilitation. Noble ideals, but unattainable. The hidden irony held within the concept of remorse is that, as a result of the prisoner's condition of confinement, he cannot find true remorse for his victim because remorse for himself continually gets in the way. Therefore, true remorse for the victim can only be achieved when the prisoner frees himself from the condition that has made him remorseful for himself. As regards rehabilitation, it is defined as the method to restore something, or someone in this case, back to a former condition. So, the African still held captive in Massachusetts has to be restored back to his former condition of slavery. Rehabilitation to the DOC and the parole board, then, is not about vocational training …academic achievement… program involvement…nor individual creativity as the means toward successful reintegration and survival in mainstream society; rather, it is about restoring ignorance and servile obedience to the master—as it began in 1632 in the Baystate, and evolved as an American institution.

The Thirteenth Amendment to the United States Constitution abolished slavery in the States and Territories of America, with the exception being that slavery is permissible when exerted upon those duly convicted of a crime. The DOC is a vehicle utilized by the oppressor-elite to maintain the institution of slavery, via the mass imprisonment[7] of black males and other people of color. Once interred within the criminal justice system's beast (the DOC), the convicted[8] and their progeny are trapped within a cycle of perpetual chattel servitude to the system forever.

Notes

1. See; Michelle Alexander, *The New Jim Crow: Mass Incarceration In The Age Of Colorblindness*, (New York: The New Press, 2010); specifically, pages 58-94, for an in-depth analysis.
2. See; George Orwell, *1984*; specifically in regard to the functions of the "Ministry of

Truth," and the concept of "double-speak." Also, cf; Don E. Fehrenbacher, *Slavery, Law and Politics: The Dred Scott Case in Historical Perspective*, (New York: Oxford University Press, 1981); page 194.

3. See; Ralph C. Hamm III, *Manumission: The Liberated Consciousness Of A Prison(er) Abolitionist*, (New Jersey: Xlibris Corporation, 2012); page 160 n. 4.

4. Cf.; *Manumission*, Id., at LESSON 7, pages 87-102; for analysis of the Massachusetts parole system.

5. Cf., *Manumission*, Id., at page 173 n. 21.

6. See; John K. Simon, "Michael Foucault On Attica: An Interview," *Social Justice* 18 (3) (FALL 1991), page 27.

7. See: Becky Pettit, *Invisible Men: Mass Incarceration And The Myth Of Black Progress*; how decades of mass incarceration has concealed decades of racial inequality; specifically, pages 13-14 (New York: Russell Sage Foundation, 2012).

8. Criminal convictions are so easy to obtain in Massachusetts that a district attorney for Worchester County once asserted in a newspaper article that he could obtain an indictment, and gain a conviction, on a ham sandwich for murder in this State.

MASS INCARCERATION:
THE FIRST AND SECOND REDEMPTION

The concept of mass incarcerating black males, in the aftermath of slavery, was practiced within the southern States around 1875 during what has historically been termed the Redemption Period in America. White southern politicians of the Democratic Party created a unified white backlash against the social, political, and economic gains made by former slaves during Reconstruction. The southern Democrats created the "Mississippi Plan," or a "divine sanction for the retaking of the authority the whites had lost in the Civil War" (Lehmann, 185). In the 1880s the former Confederate States enacted "Jim Crow Laws," which were utilized to work ex-slaves on convict-farms and plantations via convict leasing (Wacquant, 385).

"Jim Crow" lasted for approximately 85 years, or until the passage of the Civil Rights Act of 1965 and the Voters Rights Act of 1970. The Civil Rights Movement of the 1960s placed racism and racial apartheid upon the world stage, and thereby forced America to look at its policies of racial segregation and inequality in the south, as well as de facto segregation in the north and all other compass points in between. At this point in history, it was Republican party politicians and their power base who sought to derail the political influence of the Democratic Party's black vote and retake the authority whites had lost during the Civil Rights Era.

Political scientist Vesla Mae Weaver argues that race played a major role in the "historic transformation of criminal justice" (Loury, 18). Weaver postulates that, "the punitive turn" toward labelling civil rights activism as criminal civil disobedience by Republican politicians and their news media "represented a political response to the success of the Civil Rights Movement" (13) and I agree. By 1980 the second Redemption in America had begun, ushered in by former President Richard M. Nixon, and followed by all proceeding Presidents through Bill Clinton.

The second Redemption began in a similar fashion as the first, by way of a media and political campaign that alleged a rise in crime and instilled fear within the mind-set of mainstream America: a fear of black males. However, as the crime rate fell, prison expansion rose, and the incarceration of black males increased. All of the aforementioned was spurred by "war on crime," "war on drugs," and "tough on crime" rhetoric by Republican and neo-Liberal politicians (Western, Reentry).

The mass incarceration of black males frenzy that began in the 1970s continues to this day. Most social scientists agree that crime was not reduced much by the en masse imprisonment of black males. The prison industrial complex has grown as an integral component of the US job market, service-related, economy. Glenn Loury offers that the prison industrial complex "employs more Americans than the combined forces of General Motors, Ford, and Wal-Mart, the largest corporate employers in the country" (Loury, 5).

Mass incarceration is now, and always has been, the means to set back any social, political, and economic advancements made by America's marginalized black population. Incarceration serves more as a middle-class economic stimulus and regulatory response to "urban poverty," than a fundamental policy to reduce crime and promote public safety. Black people have once again been stigmatized as the "other," by politicians and media, as well as by the general mainstream public in this country. Racial minorities have been reduced to chattel and by-products; they have also been rendered stock market commodities for private prison industry companies such as Corrections Corporation of America (CCA) and the Geo Group. (*In These Times*, July 2010; page 18).

In summation, the mass incarceration of people of color (i.e., those deemed other than white) has maintained a marriage between politics and a collapsed economic market (Western, 195) throughout the past 150 years or more in this country.

References

—Nicholas Lehmann. 2006. *Redemption: The Last Battle of the Civil War*, (New York: Basic Books); Chapter 2: "The Law of God and Man".

—Loic Wacquant. 2000. "The New 'Peculiar Institution': On Prison as Surrogate Ghetto," *Theoretical Criminology* 4:377-89.

—Glenn Loury. 2008. *Race, Incarceration And American Values*, (Cambridge, MA: The MIT Press).

—Bruce Western. 2008. "Reentry: Reversing Massing Incarceration," *Boston Review* July/August 7-12.

POLICIES THAT CAN REDUCE
MASS INCARCERATION

Professor of sociology at the University of California, Loic Waquant, once said that the urban ghetto is an "ethnoracial prison"[1]; which has incarcerated millions through stigmatization, constriction, and institutional encasement. The concept of mass incarceration, and the policies necessary to reverse this sociopolitical construct, must include rending asunder the policies of marginalization surrounding inner-city communities of people of color. Adequate health care policies, equitable and culturally significant education curriculums and opportunities, are all sorely needed to release the socio-economic chains that bind black people within the prison of marginalization. A policy of employment opportunity that creates low-skilled jobs that employ an able-bodied inner-city workforce is a viable solution.

On a similar front, it has been suggested by author and sociologist Bruce Western that incarceration within penal institutions could be reduced by eliminating mandatory sentences for drug offenses, as well as a return to sentencing laws that afford statutory good time credits on indeterminate prison sentences.[2] Such laws would allow prisoners to serve 85% of their sentence based upon good behavior. Coupled with the earned good time credits that can be accrued from education and program involvement and work, the addition of statutorily mandated credits of five days per month would substantially reduce the prison population.

Another aspect of mass incarceration is in the number of parolees returned to prison for minor infractions. I am in agreement with Bruce Western, that "technical violations" should be eliminated as arguments for re-imprisonment.[3] The removal of minor infractions from parolees, such as: failure to report, lack of employment (especially in a depressed economy and the impact of CORI laws), failure to undergo drug testing, and failing unethical polygraph tests without having committed a new crime while on parole; would reduce the annual incarceration rate by about 30%, according to Western.[4]

The recent political and media hyped response to the shooting deaths of a Woburn police officer and a second degree life sentence parolee in Massachusetts has once again exposed the yellow Draconian underbelly of the Massachusetts body-politic. Hysteria has led to extend parole eligibility for second degree life sentences across the board, and the granting of fewer paroles in general. Political hackery, personal bias, and mass media induced hysteria should be alleviated from parole-granting decisions. The only way to assure those ends is through the passage of legislation that abolishes the State Parole Board, and mandates presumptive parole after the service of three-quarters served on a stipulation and program completion of a prison sentence. Such an Act by the legislature would decrease prison overcrowding, release a prospective pool of working taxpayers back into society, stifle the hysteria to build more prisons (the foundation of financial construction kick backs and political graft), and expunge millions of dollars in parole board functionality and salaries (getting paid tens of thousands of dollars annually just to say "no" on parole requests); freeing up millions that can be used toward education, health care, social welfare, or the rebuilding of the infrastructure. This is especially so if presumptive parole were mandated to be applied retroactively upon currently imposed prison sentences. The effort would immediately reverse the crippling effects of mass incarceration. After the Federal Bureau of Prisons abolished their Federal Parole Authority (i.e., the federal equivalent of a parole board), which was soon followed by several progressive State governments abolition of parole boards, they successfully put presumptive parole policies into practice. Due to the historical racism and reactionary politics in Massachusetts, correctional and parole policies continue to be reflective of the Jim Crow era in United States history (circa 1880s to 1970 in the Commonwealth[5]).

Incarcerated fathers should be allowed more paternal involvement with their children, as a matter of policy. Children of the incarcerated often follow in their father's footsteps, through the ghetto-to-public school-to-prison pipeline. Mary Katzenstein and Mary Shanley of the Charles Hamilton Houston Institute for Race and Justice, Cambridge Massachusetts, have suggested that the maintaining of family ties "helps prevent recidivism, and lowers the chances of a prisoner's children engaging in criminal activity."[6] A policy that encourages imprisoned fathers to engage with their children and families, outside of the normal visiting privileges, should be adopted; especially where such a policy is cost effective and not a threat to prison security.

Finally, the issue of mass incarceration in the modern era began in the 1980s with the "war on crime" and "war on drugs"[7] rhetoric spewed by redemptionist politicians carried by a fear-mongering national news media. The rhetoric has had the impact of cajoling public opinion into the false belief that the mass imprisonment of black males is the only solution to stem a fictionalized, out of control, crime wave. The posturing of the politicos and the media is reminiscent of the 1880s and the rhetoric utilized to pass Jim Crow laws. A renewed public policy toward treatment for drug use/abuse, instead of incarceration, would greatly reduce the influx of prisoners; as well as reduce the overcrowding of prison facilities. Most drug offenses are non-violent crimes, so those presently interred for these types of offenses could be afforded early release to attend real drug treatment programs (as opposed to the in-house farce of the Correctional Recovery Academy) with little or no threat to public safety.

Notes

1. Loic Waquant, 2000, "The New 'Peculiar Institution' : On The Prison As Surrogate Ghetto." *Theoretical Criminology* 4:377-89, page 383
2. Bruce Western, 2008, "Reentry: Reversing Mass Incarceration." *Boston Review*, July/August 7-12, page 9
3. Ibid.
4. Ibid.
5. Becky Pettit, *Invisible Men: Mass Incarceration and the Myth of Black Progress*, (New York: Russell Sage Foundation, 2012); page 75
6. Mary Fainsod Katzenstein and Mary Lynden Shanley, 2008, "No Harm: What We Owe To Incarcerated Fathers." *Boston Review*, 13:17, page 9
7. Bruce Western, "Reentry," Ibid.

DEATH, PARIAH, AND THE
PRISON BODY POLI-TRICK

South American innovative educator Paolo Friere[1] said not to be a teacher. He informs us to steer away from utilizing a forceful rote education approach, but to instruct through the use of metaphors that relate to the environment and occupations of the oppressed that they can easily recognize. If this approach is not used in instructing the oppressed, then they may be put off by the often long-winded discourses that are not a valid reflection of their life experiences. Be not a preacher. Resolve to be the wayfarer upon the crossroads of the historical, political, and social landscape, who affords an appropriate direction for the lost.

Prison is a social pariah/power/feeding-frenzy, where the pariah-oppressed (be they prisoner, guard, or administrator) prey upon one another in an effort to gain a semblance of status and power by which to elevate above their associate/fellow pariah caste members. The dog-eat-dog behavior of the pariah-oppressed is mimicked from the actions and rhetoric passed on by mealy-mouthed politicians, popular entertainers, pseudo-professionals, and corporate moguls who are displayed upon national media outlets as being the acceptable paragons of culture and social virtue in America.

Although it is true that a prison functions only by the expressed consent of its prisoners, we prisoners of the Norfolk Colony expend a tremendous amount of energy tricking ourselves into accepting the hallucination that Massachusetts Corrections is a progressive state agency, and that the inmates will ever again be given an official voice in the running of the asylum. Compared to most states in this country, including the Federal Bureau of Prisons, Massachusetts Corrections is at least ten years behind. We live in the Dark Ages of Corrections. Our anguished cries for economical, technological, vocational, and social assistance to help us keep in step with the advances in the outside community resonate upon so high a frequency these days that our oppressors have ceased to hear them. Instead, our oppressors have opted to tune into the sound of ATMs within this service-related economy. Thus, for all intent and purpose, humanity has left the sound booth.

Apathy and frustration have long since settled in, especially with the realization that no matter how many so-called treatment programs one completes...advanced educational level one attains...he still will not obtain a parole release. Every ounce of blood must be sucked from the carcass before release is possible. We reside within a hapless situation that is rooted within the draconian and reactionary nature of state poli-tricks.[2] The prison body poli-trick have become too fearful of themselves and this environment of continued social marginalization, to take a uni-racial stand against the common foe—to collectively scream "No more!", to the aggrieved conditions of our institutional slavery. Rather, we take stands against one another like the proverbial crabs in the barrel - pulling one another down with each advancement for an illusory sense of freedom from our suffrage. Our illusion of struggle is reminiscent of our youth/angst, as we fought for control of the sandbox that did not belong to us, which is probably why we cling so relentlessly to the deferred dream. Some of us have resorted to adopt the role of askari,[3] placing ourselves in league with the apartheid[4] forces that are really sociopolitical amassed against us under the slogan of "Prison Reform": placing band-aids upon the festering social wound of institutional slavery, while continuing to socioeconomically exploit us, and never allowing us to be truly free.

As should be expected, there resides anxiety and hostility here in Norfolk Colony over the composition, and decision-making, of the Parole Board; especially amongst those serving second degree life sentences with a 15 year mandatory parole eligibility. The Parole Board, as an ancillary component of the prison body poli-trick, resents the pariah-oppressed. The resentment is not due to the commission of any particular crime committed against society, for which given time has been served, but because I believe that each member of the Board recognizes (or is reminded of) the social pariah that resides within themselves. They refuse to accept it, and therefore blame the pariah—oppressed for not addressing the cause of their offending as someone to avert the scrutiny off of them. The Board draws its sustenance from the public tithe and the economical essence of enslaved men and women, like succubi,[5] and maintain their social vitality through wielding power and authority at statutorily mandated parole eligibility hearings. It is at these hearings that the Board can obscure their cannibalistic propensity under the guise of public safety. Board members readily exercise their expression of power upon the pariah-oppressed through arbitrary decision-making: i.e., determining who will be granted a renewed existence in society, and who will continue to suffer through the prolonged life-sucking death of imprisonment.

Prison body poli-tricks can become lethal when coupled with race and the nature of the offense against society, used as justification for sociopathic violence—the determination that the "other's" ethnicity and crime make him more heinous than oneself. It is a conditioned prejudice that permeates American popular culture regarding the "other" (alien), which continues to play itself out in state and national politics as well as condoned and nurtured within the prison/parole setting.

On December 12, 2011 I was saddened by the Geoghanesque[6] style death of Richard Silva—an elderly convicted pedophile who was housed within Unit 4-3, and reportedly beaten to death with a rock. This was Silva's second judgement that resulted in death, as his first judgement was banishment from society—a social death that all of the pariah-oppressed are forced to endure. Richard was another victim of many of the prison body poli-trick...forced to occupy the lowest level in the pariah-oppressed caste system. He was a flesh and blood symbol upon which to vent a collective expression of powerlessness upon. To some, the ability to either literally or figuratively take a life is a god-like expression, much like the power wielded by the judiciary, law enforcement, the military, and the parole board.

Damned if he dies, and most assuredly damned if he survives, the cycle of power continues to frenzy and feast upon the pariah-oppressed. Richard Silva's death should resound as a knell to the prison body poli-trick, bringing an end to the in-house power cycle that we practice against each other. Unfortunately, we will undoubtedly attempt to siphon-off any remnant of power that each of us can salvage from the murder—justifying the askari's excuse, and blaming the victim for his own death, because Silva lacked caste status.

Aluta Continuaa!

Written/submitted by

Ralph C. Hamm III

Notes

1. Author of such books as: *Pedagogy Of The Oppressed*, and *Education For Critical Consciousness*.

2. Be aware that fascism arises from the will of the people in a liberal democratic society. See; *The Mass Psychology Of Fascism*, by Wilhelm Reich.

3. "Askari" were black South Africans who were once members of the African National Congress, but for gratuities aligned themselves with the white apartheid government during the imprisonment of Nelson Mandela. The askari maimed and killed members of the ANC for their white masters. Winnie Mandela stepped in as leader of the ANC during her husbands interment on Robbins Island, and when her forces captured an askari they would bind him and kneel him down in the township square with a truck or automobile tire filled with gasoline around his neck, and set him ablaze.

4. "Apartheid" means any system or practice that separates people according to race, caste, or other social means.

5. "Succubi," plural of succubus—typically a female demon that drains the life force from men through intercourse while they sleep. In this day and age even demonology must be politically correct, so a succubus can be male living off of the life force of others.

6. "Geoghanesque" is a word that I created, and refers to the strangulation death of elderly pedophile priest John Geoghan within Sousa-Baranowski prison in 2002. He was also killed by a sociopath from the pariah-oppressed caste of the prison body poli-trick.

PRISON-BASED GERRYMANDERING

In 1812, Governor of Massachusetts, Elbridge Gerry's political party restructured the State's districts from the fancied resemblance of the map of Essex County to that of a salamander. Thus, the term "gerrymander" was born. To gerrymander means to divide a State, county, etc., into election districts as the means to give one political party a majority in many districts while concentrating the voting strength of the other party into as few districts as possible.

Historically, Massachusetts has always managed to be in the forefront: first to devise and institute perpetual slavery, first to institutionalize the concept of racism in the colonies, first to oppress indigenous people on the continent (i.e., Native Americans), first in injustice, and first in political corruption in America. Yet, Massachusetts was last to accept Native Americans as citizens of their own country until obligated to in 1922, and one of the last States to end Jim Crow election policies— forced to abandon literacy testing of blacks as a prelude to voting, with the passage of the Voters Rights Act in 1970.

In the 1980s came the new cause in the mass incarceration of black males in this country, and with it came the effect of political parties in the states dividing up their districts around large penal institutions. Those warehoused within these prisons are tallied as residents of the suburban city, town, county, or district in which the prison is built, and are not counted as representative of the urban area from whence the prisoner originated and would ultimately return upon release. Although most States have banned prisoners from voting, the incarcerated still must pay taxes (taxation without representation), and their bodies are utilized to inflate polls to afford additional political clout in suburban prison towns at the expense of citizens who reside in districts that do not have large prison populations. For example, if 15% of a district consists of prison inmates, then the remaining 85% of the district's population has the same political clout as 100% of the citizens in a district that does not have a prison. The effect of this practice is called: prison-based gerrymandering.

Becky Pettit expresses in her new book[1] that mass incarceration has two effects in understanding political participation by black men.

"First, it narrows the electorate by reducing the number of eligible voters through various felon disenfranchisement laws. Second, it contributes to the growing sample selection bias associated with the exclusion of inmates from household-based sample surveys of the population used to generate accounts of the voting eligible population" (77).

The Prison Policy Initiative[2] has now added a third effect of political voting manipulation due to the disproportionate mass incarceration of black men, which arises in gerrymandering schemes that are principally utilized by both major political parties to pad targeted suburban districts to the political disadvantage of suburban districts that do not have prisons and urban minority communities.

In the Crossroads Correctional Center located in the State of Maryland, an initiative to end prison-based gerrymandering was drafted and forwarded to the Maryland Chapter of the NAACP for presentation at the 101st National Convention, where it was ratified. It remains to be seen if the Massachusetts Chapter of the NAACP will take a similar step forward, and add its voice to a national initiative to end the practice. State and county legislatures around the country should be encouraged to refuse to credit prison districts with the incarcerated population. It is my belief that Massachusetts still entices suburban towns to accept the construction of new prisons in their borders based upon employment opportunities, and the garnered political clout achieved by counting prisoner heads in the district's electoral polls. Prisoners are shuffled from suburban prison town to suburban prison town like cattle across the State, for the benefit of these suburban prison towns and the detriment of the urban communities of the prisoner origin.

Maryland has already passed a "No Representation Without Population Act," which counts prisoners as residents of their legal home address for the purpose of redistricting, to adjust for decades of diluting the votes of Maryland's residents who did not live near the prison complex in western Maryland—a negative effect upon the African-American communities that experienced a disproportionate rate of imprisonment. Since then, New York, Delaware, and California have passed similar versions of the law.

Over 100 known rural counties and municipalities across the country have refused to use their prison district counts to bolster head counts for political advantage. Connecticut, Illinois, Minnesota, New Jersey, and Oregon have active reform campaigns underway.

If history is indeed an indicator, Massachusetts—whose suburban prison town populations disproportionately represent men of color from urban inner-cities by political design and intent—will hold out as a final bastion for the political incentive of prison-based gerrymandering in rural counties within the State...unless moved legislatively by its citizens to do otherwise.

Notes

1. Becky Pettit, *Invisible Men: Mass Incarceration And The Myth Of Black Progress*. (New York: Russell Sage Foundation, 2012).

2. For further information on prison-based gerrymandering, and what can be done, please contact: Prison Policy Initiative, P.O. Box 127, Northampton, MA 01061.

PAROLE BOARD:
A CALL FOR ABOLITION

On November 28, 2012 I will have served forty-four years in prison for a non-capital first offense that occurred when I was 17 years old in 1968. I am currently serving a second degree life sentence.

In "Mississippi,"[1] the only method by which a State prisoner convicted to serve a second degree life sentence can obtain a release from imprisonment is via a Massachusetts General Law, chapter 127, section 133A mandated parole eligibility hearing after having served fifteen years on said sentence and being afforded a parole certificate from the Parole Board. Uniquely, I received my first parole eligibility hearing in 1999, after having served 31 years in prison, due to the blatant misuse of the aggregation law in this State by the Parole Board. The "Mississippi" State and federal judiciary determined, by way of focus-shifting away from my central Constitutional arguments of a violation of equal protection and due process of law (the 14th Amendment to the U.S. Constitution), that "all roads lead back to Rome"—furthering the premise that a black man has no Constitutional rights that whites are bound by law to respect;[2] as regards a statutorily mandated parole eligibility hearing in 1983—after having served fifteen years on a second degree life sentence.

Due to the fact that I had the audacity to challenge the Parole Board's misuse of the aggregation policy in court, I have been penalized by the Board with 25 years of parole request denials. This fact was made evident during the course of my 2004 parole eligibility hearing, when the assistant district attorney for Essex County told the Parole Board to deny my request for parole because I appealed my conviction (something else that I assumed was a right under the 14th Amendment to the U.S. Constitution) and that I took the Parole Board to court claiming I had rights. I did indeed receive a parole request denial, and another five year review...premised upon disciplinary reports from the 1970s.

During the proceedings in my September 15, 2009 parole eligibility hearing, my lawyers[3] brought my juvenile-at-the-time-of-the-crime status to the attention of the board, through an affidavit submitted by psychologist Staci Gruber and hearing testimony. The response from the

Chairman of the Parole Board, Mark Conrad,[4] was to ask if I was a man of my convictions (beliefs). When I replied that I try to be, he quipped: "Then why don't you die in prison."; and I received another denial on my request for a parole, with a five year review (or set back). Once again, the Board relied upon disciplinary reports from 1970s Walpole Prison for the basis of their denial. The 1970s was a time in Walpole when there was 22 murders in one year, making it the most dangerous prison (per capita) in America. Prisoners were forced to fight for their lives, and the last thing that we concerned ourselves with was disciplinary reports. We lived under the basic instinct of resistance and survival. Most of the prisoners who committed the murders in Walpole Prison have since received paroles. I will be 64 years old at my next parole eligibility hearing in 2014, or I will be dead.[5]

Today, in the wake of the United States Supreme Court decisions in both Graham v. Florida (2010) and Miller v. Alabama (2012), the mental capacity of juvenile offenders during the commission of crime has finally been recognized in jurisprudence. The Court has determined that juvenile offenders can no longer be sentenced to life without the possibility of parole. They have taken into account that a juvenile does not have the same mental capacity, nor culpability, as an adult offender. As the juvenile ages he is more susceptible to rehabilitation, because he is less incorrigible.

The Committee for Public Counsel Service (CPCS), Juvenile Appeals Division, is attempting to work out a sentencing solution with "Mississippi" courts pertaining to those juvenile offenders serving natural life sentences without the possibility of parole for capital offenses—to where they can be resentenced and not faced to endure a lifetime in prison under the onus of a life sentence. However, no action is being taken in the Commonwealth to address the onus of life imprisonment faced by juvenile offenders who have not committed a capital offense, as the mandate held within Graham, Id., has been construed to be a mere suggestion. Those presently serving a natural life sentence for murder may realize a far better outcome in their resentencing than those juveniles presently serving second degree life sentences for non-capital first offenses, and God Bless them. CPCS has attempted to convince me that my serving 44 years on a non-capital second degree life sentence for an offense that occurred when I was 17 years old, and being told by the Parole Board (not as an individual, but as a State entity) to die in prison for my beliefs, is not a unique circumstance. I believe that it is. For, if not unique for the Parole Board to literally amend second degree life sentences of juvenile offenders into natural life sentences by telling them to die and then repeatedly denying their requests for parole until they do die, then the question arises as to why defense attorneys in the Commonwealth have not aligned themselves against the Parole Board and petitioned the legislature and the Governor regarding this obvious abuse of discretion. I will tell you why. When you are black in "Mississippi," no matter how young at the time of the commission of your crime, no sentence or extrajudicial amending of your sentence by a State agency is excessive or abusive. There will be no outcry of foul play.

It is possible that "Mississippi" judges will conclude that juvenile offenders serving natural life sentences should be resentenced to a second degree life sentence, which would afford a fifteen year possibility of parole. This would mean that those juveniles will be tasked to face the vindictiveness and duplicity hallmarked by the ex-prosecutor[6] and former law enforcement manned State Parole Board. If the Board can alter a second degree life sentence into a natural life sentence for a juvenile offender of a non-capital offense by telling him to die in prison, in spite of obvious rehabilitation on the offender's part, then those juvenile offenders resentenced by the court from natural life to life in the second degree do not stand a "possibility of parole." Much like the sentence of the non-capital offender, their sentence will remain one of natural life due to continual denials for parole and five year reviews, ad infinitum, under the "Mississippi" Plan.

The only viable answer to the political and media-hyped Draconian[7] nature of the Parole Board, is to encourage the State legislature into abolishing the Board and to enact a law to replace it with presumptive parole in sentencing; similar to the Federal Bureau of Prisons, and other enlightened States in the country. Neo-liberal "Mississippi" must be dragged kicking and screaming out of the dark ages of crime and punishment, and into the age of enlightenment.

Notes

1. "Mississippi" is a term that I substituted for Massachusetts, and first utilized in my 1974 poem Ameriklan Just-us (Mississippi-style), and later published in my 1979 collection of poetry, *Dear Stranger/The Wayfarer*. (New London, CT: Little Red Tree

Publishing, CT 2014).

2. SEE; Dred Scott v. John Sandford, _____Howard_____ (1857).

3. Attorneys John Swomley and Eric Tennen, Swomley & Associates.

4. Although a so-called black man, he had the habit of telling black prisoners serving second degree life sentences, who survived 1970s Walpole Prison, to die in prison; while catering to whites from the same era. A true askari of the apartheid government.

5. The last time that I checked the statistics pertaining to the life expectancy of black males in this country, it was 64 years.

6. Ex prosecutors that vie for chairman positions on the Parole Board are ambitious, and use their chair (along with the lives of the prisoners) as a political stepping stone to a future life appointment as an Associate Justice of the Superior Court.

7. Draconian means rigorous, unusually severe or cruel.

"IT'S YOUR GOOD TIME, SO HAVE A GOOD TIME"
(Fred Butterworth, former Supt., M.C.I. Walpole)

The road to reform is a solitary, harrowing, journey. It begins with an honest realization, followed by a conscious decision, that one's life is in need of a drastic overhaul. The metamorphosis arises from within the innermost recesses of the self and, after years of determination, ultimately manifests itself as a total renovation of being. It is easy to speak of change, but reform results as a matter of self-awareness.

Reform is not rehabilitation. The latter means to restore someone or something back to its former state of being. In the case of a criminal offender, rehabilitation infers that said offender must be returned back to a status of self-consciousness and social understanding prior to committing his or her criminal offense. I, for one example, have not remained mentally stagnant to the degree where rote behavioral modification systems will be able to return me to the state of being a black 17 year old male in 1968 American society. Reform, on the other hand, means to reshape or restructure. Reform is the concept that I will hereinafter utilize in terms of describing meaningful alteration to a criminal offender's sense of self-awareness and self-worth.

Correctional programs that are structured to facilitate rehabilitation by offering "good time" credits, or other forms of inducement or coercion, to garner participation from prisoners, have two major flaws that predestine reversion therapy to fail in its designed purpose. First, the salaried program facilitators are hired from the outside community—from neighborhoods and lifestyles that are typically foreign to the prisoner/participant. These program facilitators usually draw their references and beliefs from textbooks, but not from actual life experience. Their belief systems are grounded upon an educational experience that does not correlate with the life experiences of those they have been hired to instruct using rote behavioral modification techniques, and therefore their instruction is not taken seriously by the prisoner/participants. Secondly, the participants learn prior to engaging themselves in the program that in order to earn "good time" credits toward their earlier release from prison that the only requirements are to maintain their attendance and memorize the tenets of the program.

Yet, reform cannot be instructed nor forced, coerced, nor induced. Rehabilitation on the other hand, can be cajoled and induced; otherwise, there would probably be no program participation. Prisoners who are serving time under the onus of a life sentence cannot apply "good time" credits to their sentence structures, and thereby effect early release from prison, due to the determinant nature of a life sentence (a mathematical impossibility). Therefore, coercion or negative reinforcement methods are used to compel program compliance. However, rehabilitation by force never works. Unfortunately, I know of no other viable replacement for this existing system.

Prison classification boards, parole boards, and program review boards often do not know anything about a given rehabilitation program outside of its set parameters when questioning a prisoner/ participant on what he has learned. If the prisoner is honest, he may say that he has not learned anything, because his participation was either coerced or induced by the lure of earned "good time" credits being applied to his sentence. However, it is more likely that the prisoner has used the rote system to memorize the principles and tenets of said program, and has been made aware of the predictable questions that he will be asked by the board. The prisoner's awareness is garnered from his peers who have previously graduated and have attended hearings of the aforementioned nature.

Thus, most graduates of correctional rehabilitation programs leave as experienced con artists and master manipulators. Those who actually take something away from the experience to enhance their evolution, usually began their transformation long before they were induced to enroll. Remember: real change arises from the ability to incorporate life's lessons into one's very being via self-motivation. Reform is not an explanation, it is expressed as a positive attitude toward all of life in general. Reform involves critical thinking, not rote behavioral modification.

Reformed peer counsellors, or coordinators, can be seen moving throughout urban communities as street workers in their efforts to reduce crime and stem gang-related violence. They are typically ex convicts who are ex gang members, whom the present gang members have come to idolize based upon the former's street credibility. These ex gang-bangers attempt to give counsel to the youth about the errant path that was taken in their youth, and the resultant encounter with the criminal justice system. The youth tend to listen, and many may alter their destructive course.

The above can also be said about the prison environment and its programs. The 1970s was a time in prison when the road to reform was not paved with coercion and treachery. Prisoners created the programs in existence then for prisoners, and titled them: "self-help." The programs existed to assist those prisoners who made the conscious decision to change on their own, and the peer facilitators aided them in the transition.[1] The participants actually appreciated the fact that their fellow prisoners were concerned enough about their reformation to have created programs to assist them along their way. I began my transformation during the 1970s era of reform. Today, when compelled to attend correctional rehabilitation programs, I participate on the hope that my life experience of 45 years in prison; can somehow enlighten another prisoner embarking upon the journey. I do not learn slogans or spout tenets. By removing the true self-help dynamic and focusing upon flawed risk assessments, facilitator salaries, and enrollment numbers, rehabilitation programs have been reduced to promoting correctional pseudo-science aimed at garnering funding to enhance burgeoning correctional budgets, at the expense of both the prisoners and the taxpayers.

However, most prisoners will return to society with or without the application of "good time" credits to their sentence structures. Whether or not they recidivate as a result of committing a new crime has less to do with the content of a correctional rehabilitation program[2] than it rests upon a conscious decision to reoffend. "Good time" credits may aid in the early release of prisoners who, through rehabilitation, have been restored to their former selves; but they may lack the realization of fundamental reform.

Albert Einstein has been credited to have said, and here I am obligated to paraphrase:

...only a fool continues to repeat the same exact thing over and over again, and expects a different result.

This rings true in regard to the development of, and the coerced or induced participation in, correctional rehabilitation programs; as well as with those who consciously decide to return to prison.

Notes

1. Some correctional programs do utilize the services of prisoner-peers within their formats, but those peers are not there to offer their unsolicited advice and leadership— they function under the oversight and total direction of the outside facilitator and the Department of Corrections. Also, their peer services fall under the lure of earned "good time" credits.

2. Because a prisoner elects not to attend a rehabilitation program does not make him a high risk to reoffend. Not everyone needs to be programmed, but almost all can use the earned "good time" credits to reduce their time spent in prison.

MASSACHUSETTS DEPARTMENT OF CORRECTIONS
THROWS PRISONERS' VISITORS TO THE DOGS

We are responsible for the harm that results from our failure to act.[1]

In its ongoing effort to criminalise the poor as an "untouchable" caste in American society, and to further enhance the mass incarceration of said caste in this country, the Massachusetts ("Massissippi") Department of Corrections (DOC) has embarked upon another campaign to alienate its wards from their family and friends base in the community.[2]

It is my belief that a page has been excerpted from the old apartheid regime that once governed South Africa, through the country's use of "askari." Askari, in this instance, is a black person who will either sabotage or undermine the economical and social aspirations of his people (the political minority) to curry favor from the social majority. "Massissippi"—style oppression and terror has always utilized the same ilk of individuals to promote its neo-fascist agendas.

It has been the sordid history of repression and injustice in the United States to recruit and deploy compliant elitist-social-agenda enforcers (who are promised the privilege to partake of the public tithe) in an effort to further marginalize and suppress their own ethnic group, for the economic-political agenda of the power-elite.

The perverted logic of politics in America is such that if a media-generated appearance is projected to the mass consumer portraying black people destroying the lives of other black people and the poor, then there will not arise any public backlash or outcry. Thus far, for the most part, this ploy has worked to the advantage of the forces of apartheid in their partnership with the mass media. The poor are targeted because they have the least political clout, being those in a socio-economical caste who will unlikely be able to focus public attention and empathy upon the policies and practices of the DOC to thereby bring political influence to bear in the matter.

Around 2010, Commissioner of Corrections, Luis Spenser (an askari) and his department initiated a pogrom to criminalize, vilify, and annihilate the character and reputations of the families and friends of State prisoners through a policy which mandated its wards to afford the

DOC ten names (along with all aspects of personal data) of visitors to be placed upon a pre-approved list.

Once this information was gathered it was to be stored upon a DOC computer file accessible by the Massachusetts Department of Public Safety and the Federal Department of Homeland Security; thereby surrendering prisoners' families and friends to unwarranted record searches by these departments as possible threats to public and national security (a means to justify more funding), through classification as potential or probable homegrown terrorists due to their visiting State prisoners.

Based upon the outrage of prisoners' visitors, who brought their just grievances to the State House, Governor Duval Patrick (yet another askari) was forced to override the DOC mandate out of fear that negative media attention and a possible tarnished public image would hurt his political aspirations. Undoubtedly, the majority in the contingent of protestors at the State House was white; otherwise they would not have gained an audience with the Governor who caters to the majority of the voting political constituency that elected him into office.

Today, the DOC has initiated yet another pogrom against the poor families and friends of prisoners, in an effort to shift attention and focus away from its employees. Over the past three years there has been an influx in the quantity of drugs and cell phones into MCI Norfolk, and I suppose within other prisons of the Commonwealth as well. The source of large quantities of drugs and all of the cell phones can be directly attributed to DOC employees; I know of at least four staff members of MCI Norfolk that have been removed from the facility by Inner Perimeter Security (IPS). The DOC has decided to answer the call for stricter drug policy enforcement (and, of course, to solicit more public funding to enhance its bureaucracy) by placing the focus entirely upon prisoners' visitors.

Toward that end, the Commissioner has introduced a policy to use drug-sniffing dogs to determine whether prisoners' visitors are introducing contraband into State prisons. But, I believe, State employees (another viable source) are to be exempted from this intrusion. The Commissioner claims that his use of drug sniffing dogs is designed to aid in a prisoner's reentry back into society, promote public safety, and thereby strengthen family ties. It is hard to discern through this warped sense of logic how the intrusive use of canines upon innocent women and children visitors to "Massissippi" prisons can be construed as a bonding method for poor families. In actuality, it serves as a terror tactic (most inner-city residents fear police dogs, as they have been utilized as a weapon against them since slavery in this country), and a means to sever family ties by making a visit into "Massissippi" it prisons more of an ordeal than usual. It has been the history of the "Massissippi" DOC to erode and destroy any programs, to include attacks upon visitation that promotes the concept of family.

Drug sniffing dogs are not machines; therefore they are extremely fallible. Dogs have minds of their own: they have their own desire,[3] which often come into conflict with the objective of identifying whether or not drugs have been present on a given individual. A dog is able to discern the feelings of its handler, whom it is eager to please, and will afford a false positive response to the presence of drugs based upon the handler's emotions in any given set of circumstances. According to Sherry F. Colb:

> "A dog, in other words, has a mind with the capacity to take in a great deal of information about his or her environment. When people train a dog to 'sniff' narcotics, much of the training thus has to do with the dog's communicating to the handler a specified subset of the information that the dog detects. A dog, in other words, has the ability to both detect and convey to humans other information that may have nothing whatsoever to do with narcotics or criminal activity more generally."[4]

This can lead to a false positive. The dog can tell whether a positive alert to the presence of drugs is pleasing or disappointing to the dog's handler, and often opts for the pleasing result rather than to reality.

Many experts say that often dog/officer teams are inadequately handled and trained, which leads to unjustified searches. Drug sniffing dogs' false alerts and errors bring their accuracy below 20% in the real world outside of their training facilities.[5] A handler can also transfer his emotional state and biases through the leash to the dog and trigger a false alert, and an unwarranted search.

I have spoken to some MCI Norfolk prison guards about the dog drug sniffing policy, and to a man it is their belief that the Commissioner is instituting the policy to get at them. It would seem that there is a stipulation in their union contract that prohibits the DOC from subjecting the staff to any unreasonable intrusion, as a group, that prisoners' visitors are not subjected to.

I am also informed by these same guards that the dogs may be used against them on a random basis, where no doubt they will be notified in advance by their peers-the dog handlers. Whereas, families and friends of prisoners will be subjected to the indignity and biases of the dog handlers every day of the week, when there are scheduled visits to the prisons. If this is indeed the case, then one can clearly see how the DOC really views prisoner visitors and subsequent family ties-not as a viable resource to a prisoner's reentry back into society- but as consequential collateral damage in a DOC effort to destabilize the guard's union.

It has been rumored over the past year that the DOC have canines that are trained to recognize, and sniff out, the circuitry in cell phones. Since the department has determined a prisoner in possession of a cell phone to be a severe breech in security and a possible escape risk, then the detection of these phones should be a primary target for the dogs. However, as much as the DOC likes to blame prisoners' visitors for bringing these devices into the prison, it is nearly impossible for them to do so; and is a distinction in smuggling reserved only for prison employees.

A few years ago I recall an expose conducted by the "20/20" television news program, which found that 85% of the nation's paper currency in public circulation was tainted by cocaine, as rolled ten and twenty dollar bills were frequently used to snort the drug into the nose. It is therefore safe for me to say that most inner-city denizens handle paper money on a daily basis more than credit cards, due to poor credit ratings. Most state prisoners come from the inner city, as do their visitors. It stands to reason that false positives for narcotics will be frequent in regard to inner-city families and friends due to the aforementioned facts depicting the tainted nature of the country's circulating money supply.[6]

The DOC is well aware of the truth concerning the nation's money, because it was the same data that forced them to cease to use chemical swabs on visitors of prisoners to their super maximum security prison in Shirley, Massachusetts several years ago. The same drug residue that they found when chemical swabs were used on visitors will obviously be detected by drug sniffing dogs, resulting in false-positive alerts, unnecessary strip searches of prisoner visits, humiliation, character assassination, and vilifying of family and friends. Visitors who refuse to be strip-searched are barred for a year; and as a consequence of this indignity family and friends refuse to visit the prisoner.

According to Edwin Sutherland and Donald Cressey, in their textbook *Criminology*, 9th Edition (Philadelphia: Lippinscott, 197), page 133:

> "Numerous studies have shown that African Americans are more likely to be arrested, indicted, convicted, and committed to an institution than are whites who commit the same offenses, and many other studies have shown that blacks have a poorer chance than whites to receive probation, a suspended sentence, parole, commutation of a death sentence, or pardon."[7]

and this especially holds true in "Massisippi," where the prisons are bursting at the seams with young Black male prisoners. So, it should be easy to discern that these new policies of the D.O.C. are not focused on reentry, but upon the poor prisoner population in general who are sentenced to long prison terms and/or life in prison.[8]

Notes

1. Jeffrey Reiman, *The Rich Get Richer and the Poor Get Prison*, 8th ed. (Boston. Pearson, Allyn & Bacon, 2007), 76.

2. American criminal law, and its prison industrial complex, undermines the families of the poor and disenfranchised by making it more difficult for the imprisoned to maintain family ties, obtain an education, and secure meaningful employment (vocation) upon release from prison. The system deprives ex-prisoners of the right to vote, in most states, which has a catastrophic impact upon poor communities by stifling the ability to participate in the political process.

3. There is evidence where a drug-sniffing dog gave his handler a false detection of narcotics to institute an unwarranted search, so that the dog could retrieve a ball that the suspect had in his possession that belonged to his own pet. *Constitutional Law*, October 31, 2012; Sherry Colb, "The U.S. Supreme Court Considers Dog Sniffs and the Fourth Amendment," Part Two.

4. Ibid.

S. Mark Derr, "Does the Dog Know What Its Nose Knows?" *Psychology Today*, November 4, 2012.

6. Justice Souter of the U.S. Supreme Court recognized reports concerning drug residue on circulating U.S. currency, which could lead to false detection of drugs on law abiding citizens who happened to handle the money, and unwarranted searches.

See "The U.S. Supreme Court Considers Dog Sniffs and the Fourth Amendment."

7. Jeffrey Reiman, *The Rich Get Richer and the Poor Get Prison*, 8th ed. (Boston. Pearson, Allyn & Bacon, 2007), 112.

8. On a related issue, Massachusetts Parole Board statistics have repeatedly shown that white prisoners on average receive 60% of all paroles granted by the Parole board, while blacks receive an average of 21% of the granted parole certificates. The former Chairman of the Parole Board, Mark Conrad (still another askari) sympathized with white prisoners who survived 1970s Walpole State Prison and had served 30 years or more in prison on capital offenses (regardless of their institutional history) and often awarded them certificates of parole; while he regarded with contempt those black prisoners who survived 1970s Walpole Prison with over 30 years served upon their sentence for non capital offenses (especially if they were juveniles at the time of their offending) and perversely instructed them to die in prison. Today, the Parole Board affords hardly any paroles, unless the parole is to immigration and a parolee is to be deported out of the country, which leaves the overwhelming bulk of poor prisoners languishing for extensive periods of years within "Mississippi" prison cells. Therefore, the DOC excuse, concerning the reentry of prisoners to the community, as a basis for their dog drug sniffing policy, fails.

CHAPTER VI

POETRY

FEAST OF THE BEAST FROM THE EAST

From my moment of conception,
'til this time that I be,
I've been declared a virus
within the mainstream—
a marginalized social anomaly.
I've been predestined by his religion,
yet declined through his-story—
a "game boy" server drone,
charged, and "eveReady."
They installed in me a program
that says "right makes might,"
with no bypass to override
might makes right if white.
I'm played by politicos
bought off and paid for
with the lean mean green,
who appear in 2D
and talk in abstracts
upon my monitor screen.
Some gamers are askari
who betray reality, family, friends,
for special p.c—caste recognition,
and elusive apartheid dividends.
Their utility to the master-controller
is unexpected when it appears—
a sudden stab in the back, or
severance slice to spite their ears.

They've stolen my culture,
my legends, and true name.
They've stolen my pride,
and given me their shame.

They've stripped me of
manhood—
nude for all the world to see.

They'll rob me to the grave,
then tell me that I'm free.

I remember
running through the streets
as a lost and troubled youth—
clinging to the lie,
yet vying for the truth.
I remember
stumbling through my childhood
being tracked throughout my teens,
with a sound boom hovering above me
to byte upon my screams.
So, it's not by chance
"prison" is the studio version game—
an evil that alters nature
in God's name, profaned...
scheduled reruns of my tomorrows,
then rewind back to one—
an obscenity of sorrow,
cursed people of the sun.
They direct me to be cool,
and freely play along this way,
but from experience I understand
that when I play
          I pay.
I am damned if I don't
and damned if I do,
so, if I succumb to their damnation
let the muthers suffer too.

They've stolen my eyes
and all my other senses.
They've robbed me blind,
then caged me within fences.

The tragic lessons from distressing
within a man made cage,
are decades of repression
under a mad man's rage.

They say:
in idle hands
there ain't no satisfaction.
I say:
in idle minds
there ain't no serious action.
When I woke up
to find I was dead,
that I had never been alive,
I found several conscious reasons
not to accept this jive:
a people sorely taxed financially,
mortally foreclosed, socially evicted,
senate and house recognized
as thrice struck after convicted—
draconian shouts of "public safety!", tally
politico advancement, media tales, and crooks,
barbed wire, steel bars, service economy,
jim crow laws upon the books.
Taxation without representation is
a foreword for revolution.
Cross "occupy" picket lines,
                    to resign
under a neo-fascist resolution.

> They've stolen my culture,
> ancestral legends and true name.
> They've stolen all my pride,
> and replaced it with their shame.
>
> They've stripped me of my innocence—
> crude for all the world to see.
> They siphoned off my essence,
> then said: "Now you are free."

I put down
the picket sign, and
picked up the picket post
to shatter the graven image

of a father, son, and holy ghost.
They institutionalized
the blasphemy of meekness
to inherit the dirt,
and to suffer unto heaven
upon their hell on earth.
I am shaken
by the blue to my left,
crying the blues
during the night.
I stand
stirred and perturbed—rocked
black and blue from my plight.
Yet, freedom was never obtained
through peaceful means in his-story—
those who attempt to advance
without taking a stance
die a slave to obscurity.

Injustice burns my eyes,
and sears all my other senses.
It has scarred and primed
me for a lifetime within fences.

All youth has disappeared
from this east coast sage,
consumed by Legion the Beast—
they the many who feast
upon a young man's age.

A TRUE SENSE OF IMPRISONMENT

Fear makes nations
states spend adulterous fortunes
on weapons
prisons while the citizenry
go without food
shelter
health care
education.

Fear sets ethnicity
against ethnicity
gender against gender
religion against religion.
Fear of the other
of self
of culture and custom
of science
of the universe
of nothingness
of the light
of compassion.

Fear of losing control
by letting go.
Fear of pain
where suffering is denied.
Fear of relinquishing a system
due to the possibility of a different world view...
an alternative distribution of power.
Fear of the wounded
neglected inner child.
Fear contracts physically and
spiritually constricts the soul.

Legions of the fearful
lock up social systems

the poorest castes
institutions for monetary profit;
willfully mutilate and destroy
any new-born
concept or prospect of justice.

SOUL MUSIC

The moldering remains of shattered dreams
compose me from enfolding bog,
noted cell walls staffed by screams—
lilts upon the mourning fog.
Sorrowful laments of still-born men,
resemble painful melodies in despair,
or renditions of a dirge—condemned
sing refrains 'round Legion's lair.
This soulfelt aria finds rhyme home
'bout today, tomorrow, and memory
versed lines not cleft in tune—
scaled where "why" replaces "B".

A metronome tolls the River Styx—
clocks the beat with every tick.

COMPOST ED.

Of the multiple
ravings undertaken against me,
while in service
to this life
sentence,
whereby the self was rendered
unfruitful
non-productive,
I found it necessary
for me to soften
the constrictive formulation
by simply
gently
turning the pile
guilt
pain
regret
remorse
over, to tender
a bit more Spirit
into the moldering remains
of my shattered dreams.
With retooled patience
patent
attention, I lovingly undertook
the task to extract
the grey
rocky
matter
miscellaneous
from the heap…I waited
marking time
days
months
years

lines upon circular walls
harkening the season
of replantation—to
sow again,
where societal castration
had once mutated a harvest
of mores that lacked the synthesis
refinement
to arise above all expectations, as
western alchemic additives
artificially rendered me creatively
emotionally
spiritually
impotent. Instead
of my seeds falling upon infertile
unhallowed
unharrowed
stoney
ground, they found sustaining nourishment
wrought within enriched Black Soil.
The most to do,
then,
was all that Nature required
of Herself: for me
to participate within
the regeneration of my own destiny.

CONSCRIPTED MANIFESTO

There resounds this Divine
echo within me
(just a will-o-the-wisp)
as a faint whisper of God
whose reverberations will manifest,
come what may,
as poetry.
And a prison
sorely needs a poet——someone
kenotic who experiences the life
(hears the resonance of death)
here as a bard,
then finds the inner strength
(the voice)
to chronicle it in bright
fervent
and serious expression
rapidly
delicately;
yet powerfully penned strokes.
Simple words
bleeding through the sheets
of Africa's diaspora
with pages hemorrhaging
centuries (not mere years)——the
incomparable antiquity
in need of deciphering
like hieroglyphics...
stroke by stroke
the multitudinous form
one
harmonious
readable
comprehensible whole.

METAPHYSICALLY SPEAKING...

In my dreams I follow
each and every adventure.
There are no distractions,
no commercial interruptions,
just love and fear...just
the dream itself.
It is easier
to become truly conscious in my dreams,
conscious of their accepted logic,
more so than it is
for me to be aware
of myself
when I am considered awake.

In my dreams I am
not the imprisoned soul
confined by the distorted societal
perception
distraction
alteration
of the rational mind,
mindful of imprisonment. Because
in my dreams there is
no rational mind.
Logic, in its place, is
a fright-filled abstract
concept
(more a mirror than a window)
for the instability
that I isolate
hide away
in my infinitely insecure relationship
to the undream,
reality,

from which I think I am
and who I fear I am
arises.
In my dreams...

CHAPTER VII

PLAY:

REWINDING THE CLOCKWORK. ORANGE.

PREFACE

In the year 1976, I became a runner-up in the Massachusetts Council For The Arts—Artists' Fellowship Contest, in the playwright category for my play script *The Tinderbox*. Shortly thereafter, my script received a staged reading at "The Next Move Theater" in Cambridge, Massachusetts—directed and performed by James and Linda Spruill and The New African Company.

The year 1980 witnessed the maximum security prison in Santa Fe, New Mexico erupt in the worst prison riot since the 1971 one in Attica, New York. The cause of the riot was blamed upon the implementation of the Quay behavioral modification and classification system in the prison. As a result of the uprising, Massachusetts determined to implement the Quay system in Walpole State Prison where I was interred; and "Rewinding The Clockwork. Orange.," found its premise for creation.

By 1981 I had acquired a $5,000.00 promissory grant from Chris King and the Haymarket Peoples' Fund to stage "Rewinding The Clockwork. Orange.," in Walpole prison, with the assistance of Boston University student Karen Peloso. Karen had obtained permission from the university to use three student camera crews, the darkroom and editing facilities, as well as an unlimited supply of color film, to video-tape a production of the play at the prison as a school project. One week prior to the scheduled casting in the prison auditorium, the prison administration transferred me to Cellblock #10—Segregation Unit (along with fellow prisoners John Blodgett, Jake Pelletier, and Frank Stewart) on trumped-up disciplinary charges that we were planning a prisoner work strike and a taking of hostages. None of the three prisoners taken to segregation with me were a part of the play production, nor were we associates in the prison population. The unproven disciplinary allegations were the standard procedure utilized by the Department of Corrections during this period in history to set up prisoner leaders of self-help programs for transfer to the Federal

Bureau of Prisons. A multitude of prisoners from Massachusetts were transferred to the federal prison system between the years 1978-1988, most of whom upon the same trumped-up disciplinary charges using the catchall evidence: "reliable informant information."[1]

Note

1. Correctional Officer, Lieutenant Leo Bissonette, had learned of an illicit sexual relationship between Department of Corrections Caseworker Leslie McKenna and prisoner Bo Burns in Walpole State prison. Bissonette used his information to cajole McKenna and Burns to be his "reliable informants" on the false disciplinary charges levelled against myself and the three other prisoners taken to segregation. As a result, Burns and McKenna received transfers to the medium security prison in Norfolk, Massachusetts (and the two were eventually married after Burns was released from prison on completion of his sentence), and Lt. Bissonette finally received his long sought after promotion rank of Acting Captain of the guard.

PRELUDE

Every segment of this play is based upon fact—not a fabrication, nor a figment of anyone's imagination. It is reality, as it exists within the extreme environment called prison. They are situations that occur regularly and daily within my environment. The stage environment itself has been constructed to express the extreme, however, as the play itself can be construed as satyr or existentialist.

My principle reason for making the acts so short in the script was to afford a shuttering effect like a slide projector, via the opening and closing of the SCENE curtain. The second reason evolved from my desire not to expose the viewing audience (or the reader) to an overdose of the lethal insanity which fills a prisoner's every wakeful moment, as well as his nightmares.

The SIRS and MADAM wear clear plastic masks over their faces to reflect the glare of the stage lights, thus distorting their features and lending to the air of UNreality in the play.

There is also a four foot by four foot Plexiglas clock with elongated black hands that extend beyond the surface area of the clock face, located on the front of the stage outside of the SCENE curtain, but behind the stage curtain. The clock is utilized to depict the hour, in relation to the acts performed on stage. It is mechanized with huge black numerals on its face, and will have a significant role in the final scene.

CAST OF CHARACTERS

BIG SIR
Chief Supervisor of the monitors, in charge of Remote Control.

(6) SIRS
The monitors that maintain security in the Phases.

MADAM
Female monitor.

WOMAN VISITOR
Wife of the Resident with a baby.

RESIDENT
One of the imprisoned specimen in Phase Three.

INMATE
One of the imprisoned specimen in Phase Two, who accesses all
of the Phases at the behest of the monitors.

(6) PRISONERS
The imprisoned specimen in Phase One.

(3) PHASE-CONTROL PANEL MEMBERS
Remote Control's housing and classification monitors.

PRIEST
Narrator.

Direction:
KAFKAESQUE: senseless, disorienting, sometimes menacingly
complex, marked by the terror of the endless interrogation.

NARRATION BEFORE THE CURTAIN RISES

The PRIEST walks on to the stage. He faces the audience from center stage, and with Bible in hand narrates.

PRIEST

[*With feeling.*]
They say…that the Quay…system is about to begin,
with its three categories of men.
The way…of Doctor Quay…is to control a prison
through fear and racial division.
A word to the wise
interred within therapeutic designed cellblocks…
blind to the guise,
with emotions wound like clocks:
it's all fun and games played by sensory shocks.
It's a toy box!
[*The PRIEST exists the stage.*]

ACT ONE

Time: Anytime in Mississippi that the just-us system deems necessary.

Place: Social Limbo…a Phase of Incarceration Nation.

Center stage contains a three-sided enclosure, with the front open to the audience. The rear section of the enclosure is constructed to resemble the bars of a prison cell, with an open doorway right of the center. Both the right and left walls of the enclosure are of solid construction. The bars and the walls are painted white. There is a cot on the floor, the head of which is facing the audience, along the lefthand wall. The cot, the pillow, the blanket, and the sheets are all white. To the right of the foot of the cot, on the floor and close to the bars, is a white footlocker. On the floor, along the righthand wall, is a white desk - upon which is a white portable television set. Also, on the floor - with its rear even with the end of the wall nearest the audience - is a white toilet bowl. There is no sink. There are two white cardboard boxes under the cot (they contain white clothing, letters, and books) that cannot be readily distinguished by the viewing audience…as of yet.

The stage clock is set at: 1 O'CLOCK.

The stage curtain opens, followed by the opening of the orange SCENE curtain. The house lights dim, and the stage lights are lit. The soundtrack theme music from Stanley Kubrick's movie A Clockwork Orange, with a repetitive skip after the third measure, is piped through the theater sound system… loudly initially, then gradually dies down to nothingness.

Three SIRS, dressed in identical green jumpsuits, green helmets, and green boots, enter the stage through the doorway at the rear of the enclosure. [ENGAGE ORANGE STROBE LIGHT.]

SIR #1

[*Walks over to the cot, kneels, and reaches under the cot retrieving two white cardboard boxes. He tells the other two Sirs.*]
Check the footlocker and the desk.

[*He then empties the contents of the boxes on the floor.*]

SIR #2

[*Opens the footlocker, pulls everything out of it, and throws the contents on the floor.*]

Read all personal letters.

[*As he rummages through the materials on the floor.*]

SIR #3

[*Removes letters from one of the desk drawers. Opens them one at a time and reads them. He triumphantly yells.*]

Contraband!

[*And proceeds to rip the letters in half, throwing the paper on the floor. The procedure follows after reading all six letters in the desk drawer.*]

SIR #2

[*Kicks the footlocker, and then leaves the stage through the doorway he entered, leaving the contents from the footlocker on the floor.*]

SIR #1

[*Picks up a photograph album from amidst the debris on floor, and opens it.*]

Ugh...

[*Recoils in disgust.*]

Family picture! In color! Contraband!

[*He rips pictures from the album, tears them up, and throws the torn pieces on the floor.*]

SIR #2

[*Returns to the stage, through the doorway, carrying a pitcher of water. He walks over to the television set and pours the water over it. Once his task is completed, he stands and watches his confederates finish their assigned tasks.*]

SIR #3

[*His body trembling in anger.*]

What the hell is this? These are fucking legal papers!

[*He holds an open manila envelope in his hands.*]

Contraband!

[*He screams.*]

[*Walks over to the toilet and tears the envelope and its contents up, throwing the pieces into the toilet.*]

SIR #1

Let's go.

SIRS #1, #2 & #3
[*#3 and #2 pass through the doorway before #1.*]

[DISENGAGE STROBE LIGHT]

SIR #1
[*Turns around to look at the dishevelled stage. He runs over to the cot, tears the bed clothes off of it, and turns it over upside down. He walks over to the doorway and looks back over his and the other Sirs' handiwork.*]
What a mess. I'll have to write him up in a disciplinary report for his cell not being in compliance.
[*He walks off of the stage through the doorway.*]

[*Seconds pass. The RESIDENT walks on stage through the doorway of the enclosure, and stops dead in his approach. He is clad in a white jumpsuit, with white sneakers. After a few moments of what appears to be shock, he gingerly walks further into the scene—avoiding stepping upon his personal belongings. He scans the pile of debris on the floor.*]

RESIDENT
[*Bellows to the top of his voice.*]
The dirty mutha fuckers!
[*He kicks the pile of debris, pivots, and storms off of the stage through the enclosure doorway.*]

[*Stage lights dim. SCENE curtain closes*]

END OF ACT ONE

ACT TWO

Center stage contains a three-walled, orange painted, enclosure - the front of which is open to the audience. To the right of the center of the enclosure is a white, arched, walk-through, metal detector. There is a white table to the left of the metal detector. On top of the table is a red ink pad, with a large stamper labelled: VISITOR.
The hands on the stage clock turn to 2 O'CLOCK.

The SCENE curtain opens. The stage lights are brought up.

The MADAM, dressed in a green jumpsuit, green helmet, and green boots, is standing on the stage between the metal detector and the table.

The WOMAN VISITOR, adorned in a white dress, white shoes, and a white scarf, is carrying a baby. The baby is wearing a cotton diaper, and is wrapped in a white blanket. The WOMAN VISITOR is being ushered toward the metal detector by the MADAM.

MADAM
[*Waves her left hand at the visitor.*]
Just step through and over to here.
[*She directs in an authoritative manner, pointing at the table.*]

[*The WOMAN VISITOR, with the baby in her arms, walks toward the arched metal detector. Just as she reaches the middle of the archway, a siren blares. The scene is bathed in a flashing red light, and the WOMAN VISITOR looks around in terror. The MADAM runs to the end of the metal detector where the WOMAN VISITOR is quaking, grabs the woman by the arm, and practically drags her over to the table. The red light and the siren cease.*]

[ENGAGE ORANGE STROBE LIGHT]

WOMAN VISITOR
[*Visibly shaken.*]
What have I done? What is it?
[*Obvious panic in her voice.*]

MADAM

[Mechanically.]
One of you is carrying contraband.
[She wrests the baby from the arms of the Woman, and yells at it.]
You've got to be the one!
[She places the baby on the table, spins around to face the
Woman, and begins to pat search her.]

[*The WOMAN VISITOR recoils from the touch of the MADAM, as the
latter shoves her hand down the front of the Woman's dress...feeling
around.*]

MADAM

Don't move...it'll only make things worse for you!

WOMAN VISITOR

[*Closes her eyes, with a look of revulsion on her face.*]
I'm not carrying anything. Ouch!

MADAM

Don't move.
[*Runs her hands up the Woman's leg and under her dress.*]

WOMAN VISITOR

[*Tearfully pleads.*]
Please. Please stop.
[*The MADAM jerks her hand from under the Woman's dress, pivots, and
walks over to the table where the baby is.*]

MADAM

It must be you!
[*She yanks the blanket from around the baby, reaches toward the
diaper.*]
Contraband! I can see through your diaper!
[*Glares at the baby, then reaches down and removes the baby's diaper.
When she doesn't find anything else, she remarks in disappointment.*]
Nothing. But can you risk a rectal search?

[*Throws the removed diaper on the floor, turns the baby over on it's stomach, then roughly proceeds to examine the baby's buttocks. The baby begins to scream.*]

[*Meanwhile, the WOMAN VISITOR collects herself, along with the discarded belongings of the baby. She approaches the MADAM, and witnesses with horror what the MADAM is doing to her child.*]

[DISENGAGE STROBE LIGHT]

MADAM

[*Satisfied with the result of her searches, and glorified by the humiliation that she has caused the Woman.*]

You can go in now, but be prepared for a suspension.

[*She picks up the stamper from the table, opens the ink pad and presses the stamper onto it; then, imprints: VISITOR in bold red letters upon the foreheads of the WOMAN VISITOR and the baby.*]

[*The WOMAN VISITOR, in tears, scoops up her child into her arms, and takes a couple of steps toward the front of the stage. Stage lights dim. SCENE curtain closes.*]

END OF ACT TWO

ACT THREE

Center stage contains a three-walled, barred rear, white enclosure. There is a white desk and chair set on the floor inside of the enclosure, in a diagonal position near the left and rear corner of the wall. Upon the desk sits a green telephone.

The hands of the clock turn to 3 O'CLOCK.

The SCENE curtain opens. The stage lights are brought up. When the curtain opens it reveals a SIR, dressed in his green jumpsuit, sitting in the chair behind the desk. Moments of silence pass, while the SIR sits behind the desk in a rigid inanimate state. Automation begins in the SIR when the INMATE enters the stage through the doorway on the rear barred wall of the set, and approaches the desk. The INMATE is wearing a white jumpsuit and white sneakers.

INMATE

[*Walks up to the desk.*]
Morning Sir!
[*Seats himself on the top of the desk, corner front, nearest to the rear wall.*]

SIR

[*Turns his head in the direction of the INMATE, and nods his recognition.*]
Morning.

INMATE

I hear that Resident 187 had contraband in his room.

SIR

He did.

INMATE

Yeah, well he's always making it hard for himself.
[*The telephone on the desk rings.*]

SIR

[*Responds to the ringing telephone by picking up the receiver and places it to his ear.*]

132

Sir! Phase One!

    [*Shouting into the receiver. He listens intently, in silence for a few seconds, then replaces the telephone receiver on its cradle.*]

187 is up for restraint.

    [*To the inmate, as if their conversation had never been interrupted.*]

INMATE

    [*Snickers.*]

Maybe it'll do him some good this time.

SIR

    [*Authoritatively.*]

Restraint is always good!

INMATE

    [*Fidgets on his perch.*]

Oh yeah…yeah…of course.

    [*He shakes his head up and down enthusiastically.*]

    [*Silence ensues. Momentarily, he stands up.*]

Can you get me a roll of Sir toilet paper? That stuff they give us is like firewood.

SIR

    [*Gets to his feet.*]

Sure…sure, let me go to Remote Control and get some.

    [*The SIR walks out from behind his desk, and exits the stage through the doorway on the rear wall of the set. He disappears off stage. Meanwhile, the INMATE sits back down on the corner of the desk. Moments of silence and inactivity pass. The SIR returns on stage through the doorway carrying a roll of neatly wrapped toilet paper. The INMATE stands up as the SIR approaches the desk, where he is handed the roll of toilet paper.*]

SIR

Here you go.

    [*Makes his way around the desk to his chair, and sits down.*]

INMATE

[*Smiles.*]

Thank you, Sir

[*Turns around, and walks off of the stage through the doorway of the enclosure.*]

[*A PRISONER walks on to the stage by way of the enclosure doorway. He is dressed in an orange jumpsuit and sneakers, with a red "P" stencilled upon the front of the jumpsuit.*]

PRISONER

[*Upon reaching the desk.*]

I've had bleeding hemorrhoids three times this year. I can't earn the privilege of an operation 'cause I'm a Prisoner. I can't get any medical treatment, but I need some real toilet paper.

SIR

[*Sarcastically.*]

Can't help you. It's all contraband to you, Prisoner! Why don't you pay for it?

PRISONER

[*Incredulous.*]

Pay for it? I'm a ward of the State, and I'm already paying for it!

[*Becomes angry.*]

All your medical is free!

SIR

[*Amused.*]

Why don't you join a union, Prisoner? Don't bitch to me!

PRISONER

What?

[*The SIR does not respond.*]

PRISONER

[*Angrily screams at the Sir.*]

You merciless piece of shit!

[*He spins around, and stomps off of the stage through the doorway on the enclosure.*]

[*The SIR picks up the receiver of the telephone, and places it to his ear.*]

SIR

[*In a normal voice.*]

Remote Control?

[*He then shouts into the receiver.*]

Sir! Phase One!

[*Then, in a much softer voice.*]

Place Prisoner 249 on report for insolence toward a staff monitor. It was undeserved.

[*He places the receiver back upon its cradle, then becomes rigid once again.*]

[*Stage lights dim. SCENE curtain closes.*]

END OF ACT THREE

ACT FOUR

The stage clock hands turn to 4 O'CLOCK.

The SCENE curtain opens. The stage lights are brought up. The SIR is still sitting rigidly behind the desk. An orange jumpsuit clad PRISONER, different from the one in Act Three, walks onto the stage through the enclosure doorway. He is holding his stomach in obvious pain as he approaches the desk.

PRISONER

[*Slightly crouched.*]
Sir...will you call the infirmary? I've been having these stomach cramps for over two weeks, and I haven't been able to get to the infirmary yet.
[*His voice expresses the pain that he is experiencing.*]

SIR

[*Becomes animated.*]
I will call Remote Control.
[*Picks up the telephone receiver, and speaks normally into it.*]
Remote Control?
[*He then shouts.*]
SIR! Phase One!
[*Several seconds of silence ensues.*]
Prisoner 364 requests to be sent to the infirmary. I have no idea as to his condition.
[*More silence, then addresses the Prisoner.*]
Fill out Phase Order 44 dash 3.
[*Hangs up the receiver.*]

PRISONER

[*Moans, in agony and exasperation.*]
I've already done that...a hundred times.

SIR

[*Sarcastically.*]
Well, make it one hundred and one.

[*He becomes rigid again.*]

[*The PRISONER, having resigned himself to the fact that he is not going to get anything else out of the Sir, turns around and shuffles off stage through the enclosure doorway. Stage lights dim. SCENE curtain closes.*]

END OF ACT FOUR

ACT FIVE

Center stage contains a three-walled orange enclosure, with a barred rear section. Behind the barred section is an orange cot, an orange footlocker, an orange desk, and an orange toilet; all arranged to resemble the interior of a prison cell. There is a solid orange wall (or partition) located at the furthest extremity of the cell, which acts as its rear wall. All together, the scene depicts a three-walled orange enclosure, with a prison cell to its rear. The area in front of the cell depicts a cellblock common area.

The hands of the stage clock turn to 5 O'CLOCK.

The SCENE curtain opens. The stage lights are brought up, to reveal 4 PRISONERS—clad in orange jumpsuits and sneakers, with a red "P" stencilled on the front of the jumpsuit—sitting in a group on the floor of the common area, in the middle of the scene.

PRISONER #1

[*Rubs his stomach, and looks around at the others seated with him.*]
I'm starving.

PRISONER #2

[*Chuckles.*]
Right. You're always starving.

PRISONER #3

[*Stands up.*]
I've got some bread in the cell…we can make some toast.
[*He walks over to and through the doorway at the rear of the set, and into the cell.*]

PRISONER #4

[*Grimaces.*]
Man, we exist on toast.

PRISONER #2

[*Turns his head in the direction of the rear of the set, and addresses*

Prisoner #3 who is in the cell.]
Don't forget the coat hanger and that hard ass toilet paper!

[*Presently, PRISONER #3 has retrieved a loaf of bread from within the footlocker, which he tosses upon the cot. He then gets down on his knees next to the cot, reaches under it and pulls out several large sheets of cardboard and a rusty coat hanger.*]

PRISONER #1

[*Exhibiting signs of anxiety.*]
How you doing in there? What are you doing…baking the bread?

[*By this time, PRISONER #3 has all of the ingredients in his arms, and is walking over toward the other three Prisoners.*]

PRISONER #3:

[*Having reached the group.*]
All right. Here we go. Help me with this shit.

[*The other Prisoners assist PRISONER #3, by each taking a portion of his load. They place all of the items on the floor. The cardboard is passed around, and they all begin to tear it into small pieces. There is silence during this process, except for the sound of the tearing of cardboard.*]

PRISONER #4

[*Finishes tearing up his portion of the cardboard, and retrieves the rusty coat hanger.*]
This thing has seen better days.
[*He bends it in the middle, and shapes it into a "Y", so that it can hold a slice of bread.*]
Who's going to do the cooking?
[*Looks around for a volunteer. PRISONER #3 sits down with the others.*]

PRISONER #2

[*Points to Prisoner #1.*]
Let him do it. It was his idea.

PRISONER #1

[*Reaches for the loaf of bread, and begins to open the bag.*]
You're damn right. I don"t mind.

[*He directs his attention to PRISONER #2.*]
Although it was my idea, I bet you get your share.

[*They all laugh.*]

PRISONER #4

[*Hands the coat hanger to Prisoner #1.*]
Here ya go.
[*Reaches into his sneaker and pulls out a book of matches.*]

[*The Prisoners make a small pile out of the torn up pieces of cardboard,
moving the remainder of the material to the side.*]

PRISONER #3

[*Stands up.*]
I knew I forgot something.
[*Begins to walk to the rear of the set toward the direction of the cell
doorway.*]

PRISONER #1

[*Looks around at the material on the floor.*]
What's missing?

PRISONER #3

[*Walks through the doorway into the cell.*]
The damn can.

PRISONER #4

[*Seemingly perplexed.*]
The can?

PRISONER #2

[*Looks at Prisoner #4 in amazement.*]
Yeah. The can we cook in.

[*He picks up some of the pieces of cardboard.*]
Where we put the fire?
[*Shakes his head from side to side.*]
Are you here with us?

[*During the above exchange, PRISONER #3 is rummaging through the contents of the cell, cursing to himself.*]

PRISONER #4

[*Turns attention away from himself.*]
Listen to him in there…going nuts…swearing at himself.

[*They all laugh, with the exception of Prisoner #3.*]

PRISONER #3

[*Angrily yells.*]
I don't see what's so fuckin' funny! I can't find the fuckin' thing!

PRISONER #1

[*Yells back.*]
One of the Sirs probably took it!

[*A voice on the public address system blurts out.*]

VOICE

Resident 187…Resident 187…you have a visitor.

4 PRISONERS

[*In unison…loudly.*]
Fuck you, sir!

[*Stage lights dim. SCENE curtain closes.*]

END OF ACT FIVE

ACT SIX

The scene is set center stage with a three-walled white enclosure, and has the front end open to the audience. To the rear of the enclosure on stage is a green desk and chair. The desk has a green telephone on it. On the wall behind the desk, to the right, are two signs written in bold black letters. One of the signs reads: NO NECESSARY MOVEMENT; and the other one reads: THERE IS NO TOILET INSIDE - NO BOWEL MOVEMENT. To the front left center of the set is a white table with a white chair on the left and right of it.

The hands of the stage clock turn to : 6 O'CLOCK.

The SCENE curtain opens. The stage lights are brought up. There is a SIR seated at the green desk at the rear of the set, bedecked in a green jumpsuit and boots, along with a green helmet. The RESIDENT, in white jumpsuit and sneakers, is seated in the white chair to the right of the white table. The WOMAN VISITOR and her baby are seated on the left, she has the baby in her arms. The word: VISITOR is clearly visible, stamped upon the Woman's and baby's forehead.

WOMAN VISITOR

[*Tearfully.*]

Three hours waiting in the holding area to get in here!

[*Shakes her head from side to side to display her disbelief.*]

I've never been so humiliated in my life…who would believe what she did to the baby!

[*Looks down at the bundle in her arms.*]

It was bad enough what she did to me, but what she did to the baby was monstrous!

RESIDENT

[*Hands on the table, head bent in dejection.*]

I feel so helpless. What can I do when they attack my family?

[*Raises both hands in the air, pleading with the heavens, then looks directly into the eyes of the WOMAN VISITOR, to add emphasis to his feelings of helplessness.*]

No one cares. My hands are tied.

[*Drops his hands upon the table top, then drops his chin to his chest.*]

WOMAN VISITOR
[*Reaches her hand across the table and touches the RESIDENT's head.*]
I know that there's nothing you can do. It's not that important. I'm just a little frustrated, that's all.

SIR
[*In a booming voice.*]
There will be no touching!
[*The WOMAN VISITOR jerks her hand away from the RESIDENT's head. The telephone on the desk rings.*]

[ENGAGE STROBE.]

SIR
[*Picks up the telephone receiver, and shouts into it.*]
Sir! Phase Three Visitor's Tank!
[*His voice startles the other players on stage, and they look fearfully in his direction. After a few moments of silence, while he is apparently listening to the voice on the other end of the phone line, he replaces the receiver on its cradle, stands at attention, and makes a loud announcement.*]
Visit is terminated!
[*He walks over to where the Resident and Woman are seated, then points at the baby.*]
That has been classified contraband!
[*Looks at the woman.*]
Visiting privileges have been terminated indefinitely because you introduced contraband into this facility!

[*The WOMAN VISITOR and the RESIDENT stand up.*]

RESIDENT
[*Tearfully, speaking to the WOMAN VISITOR.*]
Don't come up anymore. I'm not going to put you and our baby through this.

[*The MADAM walks on stage from the front left, and escorts the WOMAN VISITOR and baby off the stage, leaving the SIR and the RESIDENT standing on stage alone.*]

SIR

[*Authoritatively.*]

Okay...strip!

[*The RESIDENT takes off his jumpsuit (under which he is wearing a flesh toned body stocking) and sneakers. He throws the items of clothing upon the table. The SIR carefully inspects each discarded item for a few moments, then turns his attention to the RESIDENT.*]

Turn around!

[*The RESIDENT complies.*]

Bend over!

[*The RESIDENT complies.*]

Spread those cheeks!

[*The RESIDENT complies.*]

Okay, get dressed!

[*The RESIDENT puts his jumpsuit and sneakers back on.*]

RESIDENT

[*Looks around.*]

Who's going to escort me back to Phase Three?

SIR:

You are not going back to Phase Three...you're going to Restraint!

RESIDENT

[*Shocked.*]

For what?

SIR

Contraband.

RESIDENT

[*In obvious bewilderment.*]

What contraband?

SIR

Contraband that was found in your housing area... contraband on your visit.

RESIDENT

[*Defensively.*]
You didn't find anything on me!

SIR

One of your visitors was contraband, and you knew it. The Phase Control Panel will review your housing and reclassify you tomorrow. They will go into the details of your restraint.

[*He grabs the RESIDENT by the arm, and walks him off stage via the right front.*]

[DISENGAGE STROBE]

[*The stage lights dim. The SCENE curtain closes.*]

END OF ACT SIX.

ACT SEVEN

Center stage is set with the three-walled, barred rear, white enclosure. There is a white cot, made up with white sheets and a white blanket, on the floor along the left-hand wall. Beside the right-hand wall, on the floor, is a white desk with a framed picture of a woman on it. On the floor, at the forward extreme of the right-hand wall, is a white toilet bowl. To the rear of the set, on the floor against the barred wall, is a white footlocker.

The hands of the stage clock turn to: 7 O'CLOCK.

The SCENE curtain opens. The stage lights are brought up to reveal a PRISONER in an orange jumpsuit and sneakers. He is pacing back and forth on the stage. He is the PRISONER from ACT THREE.

PRISONER

[*Talking aloud, to himself.*]
I can't sit down...I'm afraid to use the toilet.

[*Stops pacing, and stands looking through the bars.*]
That dirty sunnuvabitch down there at his desk don't wanna get up off a any real toilet paper! Probably wants me to bleed to death.

[*Kicks the footlocker, then begins pacing again. An interval ensues where all that can be heard is the PRISONER's pacing.*]
To hell with this walking! I need to sit down.

[*He gingerly takes a seat upon the cot, but immediately jumps back up into a standing position.*]
Shit, that hurts!

[*Tries to sit down again, this time with painful success.*]

[*A voice on the public address system erupts.*]

VOICE

Phase Three...Phase Three...chow.

PRISONER

[*Yells back.*]
Gravy Train, you mindless saps! That's what the real deal is...as quiet as

it is kept!

[*He reaches a hand over to the desk, and picks up the framed picture.*]
Hey, girl, what it be like? Ain't nothing shaking here that ain't a pain in the ass.

[*Snickers at the pun that he has made, in regard to his suffering.*]
Yeah, definitely a pain in the ass.

[*He lays the picture down on the cot next to him, stands up and looks around the stage. He then kneels down beside the cot, then reaches under it searching for something. When he brings his hand back out he is holding a sheet of cardboard. He gingerly, and painfully, sits back down on the cot, picks up the framed picture, and holds the cardboard up in front of it.*]
See, this shit I've got to deal with? This is why I am in pain.

[*Angrily throws the cardboard toward the front of the stage. The voice on the public address system erupts again.*]

VOICE

Phase Two...Phase Two...chow.

PRISONER

[*Attempting to mock the voice.*]
Phase Two...Phase Two...your mother!

[*Holds the picture in both hands in reflective silence.*]

[*The sound of many shuffling feet can be heard...as if a procession of zombies is passing by the rear of the stage, out of view of the audience. The shuffling goes on for about thirty seconds, while the PRISONER sits contemplating the picture in his hands.*]

PRISONER

[*As the shuffling ends.*]
Phase Three gets the food...Phase Two gets the leftovers. We get the scraps.

[*Sighs, then puts the picture back on the cot. Grimaces.*]
These beds are hard as shit.

[*Stands up, and begins pacing again.*]
All they think about is saving money! Can't get an operation 'cause it's a

privilege. Toilet paper is as hard as shit! Shit for food!

[*Abruptly stops pacing, and stares out at the audience.*]

Listen to me...talking to myself! I'm going nuts!

[*Rubs his temples, in torment.*]

[*Stage lights dim. The SCENE curtain closes.*]

END OF ACT SEVEN

ACT EIGHT

Center stage is set with a white three-walled enclosure open to the audience, with a barred rear wall that has a doorway. There is a green chair and desk within the enclosure positioned diagonally across the left rear wall corner. There is a green telephone on top of the desk.

The hands of the stage clock turn to: 8 O'CLOCK.

The SCENE curtain opens. The stage lights are brought up. A SIR is sitting rigidly behind the desk. The orange jumpsuit clad PRISONER from Act four walks onto the stage through the doorway at the rear of the set. He is holding his stomach, in obvious pain, and carrying a sheet of paper in his right hand. He proceeds to the desk.

PRISONER
[*Lays the sheet of paper on the desk top.*]
Sir, here is the form that I was told to fill out to get to the infirmary.

SIR
[*Becomes animated.*]
Phase Order 44 dash 2?

PRISONER
[*Confused.*]
No...Phase Order 44 dash 3.

SIR
[*Looks at the "P" on the Prisoner's jumpsuit.*]
You are a prisoner! And, you are out of Phase!

[ENGAGE STROBE LIGHT]

PRISONER
[*Angrily.*]
What the hell are you talking about, I'm out of Phase? You're the one who told me to fill out this Phase Order!
[*Picks up the sheet of paper from the desk, then throws it back down on the desk top.*]

149

SIR

[*Matter-of-factly.*]
That was earlier. I am now Sir, Phase Two.

PRISONER

[*Baffled.*]
Phase Two? This is Phase One! I live on the third level of this Phase!

SIR

Not any more. Phase One has been moved down the corridor.

PRISONER

[*Looks around, completely puzzled.*]
When?

SIR

Just now. Since you've been standing here.

PRISONER

[*Bellows.*]
What?

SIR

[*Nonchalantly.*]
Since you've been standing here.
    [*Picks the sheet of paper up from off of the desk, and hands it back to
    the PRISONER.*]
So, you see Prisoner, you are out of Phase and subject to Restraint.
    [*Two SIRS walk on stage, and stand on either side of the Prisoner, then
    grab both of his arms.*]

PRISONER

[*Struggles with the two Sirs.*]
This is crazy!
    [*The struggling Prisoner is escorted off of the stage by the two Sirs.*]

    [*They exit through the doorway at the rear of the set.*]

[DISENGAGE STROBE LIGHT]

[The stage lights dim. The SCENE curtain closes.]

END OF ACT EIGHT

ACT NINE

Center stage is set with a white three-walled, enclosure open to the audience. To the rear of the enclosure, near the left hand corner, is a green nine foot high judge's bench. On the right of the bench, approximately two feet away, is a green desk with "PCP" painted on the front of it in bold black letters.

The hands of the stage clock turn to: 9 O'CLOCK.

The SCENE curtain opens. The stage lights are brought up.

BIG SIR, a man of short stature, clad in an oversized green jumpsuit, replete with a too large green helmet and boots, is sitting behind the judge's bench. Seated behind the green desk are three individuals clad in green scrubs, cap and mask, also wearing green sneakers. The sneakers can been seen from under the desk by the audience. These are the three PHASE CONTROL PANEL members, who are jockeying each other for position at the desk. The arrival of the RESIDENT, escorted by a SIR, via the left front of the stage, stops the jostling of the Panel members. The RESIDENT is clad only in his nude colored body stocking.

[ENGAGE REVERB, AND ORANGE STROBE LIGHT]

BIG SIR

[*Looks down.*]

Welcome to Remote Control, Resident 187.

[*The SIR escorts the RESIDENT up to two feet in front of the bench, then retreats to the far right hand corner of the set and stands at attention.*]

PHASE CONTROL PANEL MEMBER #1

[*In a shrill voice.*]

You have come to be re-Phased.

PHASE CONTROL PANEL MEMBER #2

[*In a deep voice.*]

You are now in Restraint?

RESIDENT

[*Stands with his hands crossed in front of his groin, responds vehemently.*]
No! I am now standing here with you idiots!

BIG SIR

[*With a smirk on his face.*]
Don't make it worse for yourself, 187.

PHASE CONTROL PANEL MEMBER #3

[*In a childlike voice.*]
Yeah...don't be a smart ass.
[*Giggles.*]
I said ass.
[*The PHASE CONTROL PANEL MEMBERS begin goosing one another.*]

BIG SIR

[*Addresses the Panel members.*]
Will you three clowns knock it off? This is a serious matter before us.
187 has been engaged in creating contraband!

PHASE CONTROL PANEL MEMBERS

[*The three members intone in unison, while rubbing their index fingers
across one another, and shaking their heads from side to side.*]
Shame! Shame! Contraband!"

RESIDENT

[*Enraged.*]
You assholes are insane!
[*Nods his head at the Panel.*]
What are you three morons supposed to be, doctors or something?

PHASE CONTROL PANEL MEMBER #2

[*Waves a hand in the air.*]
Big Sir, Big Sir, can I answer that one?

BIG SIR

[*Smiles complacently.*]

Why not. Give it a shot.

PHASE CONTROL PANEL MEMBER #2
[*Addresses the other panel members.*]
Doctors? Who can tell. All together now.

ALL PHASE CONTROL PANEL MEMBERS
[*In unison.*]
We're insane, but you're restrained. We're insane, but you're restrained.
[*Point their fingers at the RESIDENT.*]

RESIDENT
[*Incredulous, shakes his head from side to side.*]
I don't believe this.

BIG SIR
[*In a mocking tone.*]
I don't believe this.

ALL PHASE CONTROL PANEL MEMBERS
[*In unison, mocking the RESIDENT.*]
I don't believe this."

BIG SIR
[*Laughs.*]
Look, 187, we're here to help you.
[*Looks down at the Panel members, who nod in agreement, then speaks to the RESIDENT in a soothing voice.*]
Do you have a problem, 187? Tell us. Maybe we can help you.

[DISENGAGE REVERB]

RESIDENT
[*Taken in by the apparent sincerity.*]
My wife has been suspended indefinitely.
[*Strains his neck to look up at Big Sir.*]

[ENGAGE REVERB]

BIG SIR

[*Leers.*]
Your visit was contraband!

ALL PHASE CONTROL PANEL MEMBERS
[*In unison, while rubbing their index fingers across one another, and shaking their heads from side to side.*]
Shame! Shame! Contraband!
[*The RESIDENT drops his chin to his chest, in surrender to his circumstance.*]

BIG SIR

[*Spits out.*]
The baby was contraband…was wearing contraband!
[*Looks down at the Panel members, and addresses them.*]
What is your verdict?"

PHASE CONTROL PANEL MEMBER #1
Castrate him!

BIG SIR

[*Shakes his head.*]
We've already done that, dummy!

PHASE CONTROL PANEL MEMBER #2
Degrade him in front of his family!

BIG SIR

[*Exasperated.*]
What am I surrounded by, a bunch of incompetents?
[*Looks up to the heavens, and implores.*]
God, help me.
[*Looks back at the Panel members.*]
We've already done that!

PHASE CONTROL PANEL MEMBER #3

[*Wincing.*]

Destroy all family ties?"

BIG SIR

[*Erupts.*]

Ahhhh! What the hell? We've done it!

[*Bangs his hand on the bench.*]

ALL PHASE CONTROL PANEL MEMBERS

[*In unison.*]

Indefinite Restraint!"

BIG SIR

[*Claps his hands in glee.*]

Now you've got it!

[DISENGAGE REVERB AND STROBE LIGHT]

[*The SIR, who was standing at attention against the wall, walks over to the RESIDENT and takes him by the arm. The SIR escorts him off of the stage the way that they entered. The PHASE CONTROL PANEL begin tickling and goosing one another, while BIG SIR watches them in amusement. Stage lights dim. The SCENE curtain closes.*]

END OF ACT NINE

ACT TEN

The center stage is set with a white three-walled enclosure that is open to the audience. The rear wall is barred with a doorway. There is a white chair and desk that is positioned diagonally across the left rear wall corner. There is a green telephone on the desk.
The hands of the stage clock turn to: 10 O'CLOCK.

The SCENE curtain opens. The stage lights are brought up. A SIR is sitting rigidly on the chair behind the desk. The orange jumpsuit clad PRISONER from Acts four and eight walks on to the stage through the rear doorway. He is hunched over, and clutching his stomach. There is a wrinkled piece of paper in his right hand. He approaches the desk.

PRISONER
[*In a pained voice.*]
Sir, here is the form that you told me to fill out for me to get to the infirmary.
[*Lays the paper, then rests his hands, upon the desk.*]

SIR
[*Becomes animated.*]
Phase Order 44 dash R?

PRISONER
[*Groans.*]
No. It's Phase Order 44 dash 2.
[*Places his hands on his stomach.*]

SIR
[*Notices the "P" stenciled on the Prisoner's chest.*]
You are a Prisoner in Restraint! Order 44 dash 2 is out of Phase, Prisoner.

PRISONER
[*Momentarily covers his face with his hands.*]
Oh, no not again.
[*Shakes his head from side to side and groans.*]

157

What's the difference?

SIR

You were brought to Restraint, Prisoner. This is Restraint.

PRISONER

[*Exasperated.*]

You were the Sir in Phase One that is now Phase Two, and you told me that this was Phase One but its now Restraint.

[*Takes his hands away from his face, and retrieves the paper from the desk.*]

SIR

Phase One was here. Phase Two was here. Now it's Restraint.

PRISONER

Since when?

SIR

Since you've been standing here.

PRISONER

[*Talks aloud to himself, and throws his arms in the air in frustration.*]

What the fuck is it going to take to get me to the infirmary?

SIR

Phase Order 44 dash R

[*Picks up the receiver of the telephone.*]

And by the way, you're going on report for insolence toward a monitor.

PRISONER

[*In a rage.*]

Report! Restraint! Whatever! I'm going to the infirmary now!

[ENGAGE STROBE LIGHT]

[*He snatches up the base of the telephone from off of the desk, and leaps on the Sir. They both land on the floor, struggling. The voice on the public address system erupts.*]

VOICE

Monitor Alert! Monitor Alert! Sir Squad to Restraint! Sir Squad to Restraint!

[*Running footsteps can be heard. Momentarily, five green jump-suited SIRS rush on stage through the rear doorway. They have "S.S." stenciled on their green helmets in bold white letters. They join the fray on the floor. Seconds later, having subdued the PRISONER and rendered him unconscious, the S.S. carry him off stage through the rear doorway. The Restraint SIR collects himself, and takes his seat behind the desk.*]

[DISENGAGE STROBE LIGHT]

[*Stage lights dim. The SCENE curtain closes.*]

END OF ACT TEN

ACT ELEVEN

Center stage is set with the white three-walled enclosure. The hands of the stage clock turn to: 11 O'CLOCK.

The SCENE curtain opens. The stage lights are brought up. The RESIDENT, wearing a white jumpsuit, is sitting cross-legged on the floor. He is facing the audience, and there is a red "R" stamped upon his forehead. He sits in this position in silence for a few seconds, then voices can be heard coming off set from around the stage.

[ENGAGE REVERB]

VOICES

Letters?

Contraband.

Family pictures?

Contraband.

Legal research papers?

Contraband.

Them dirty mutha fuckers!

[*The RESIDENT puts his elbows on his knees, and his head in his hands.*]

I've never been so humiliated in my life! Would you believe what she did to my baby?

I feel so helpless.

I feel so helpless.

I feel so helpless.

My hands are tied.

There will be no touching!

Visit is terminated!

Visitor privileges have been terminated indefinitely!

Don't bother coming up anymore.

Don't bother coming up anymore.

Don't bother coming up anymore.

[*The RESIDENT begins rocking from side to side.*]

Okay...strip!

Okay...strip!

The baby was contraband!
The baby was contraband!
The baby was contraband!
Do you have a problem, 187?
Do you have a problem, 187?
After all that we have done for you.
After all that we have done for you.

[*A braided orange and green rope with a noose on the end is lowered from the ceiling, and comes to a halt directly in front of the sitting RESIDENT. He lifts his head up from his hands, and sits staring at the noose.*]

[ENGAGE ORANGE STROBE LIGHT]

VOICES

Indefinite Restraint!
Indefinite Restraint!
We're insane, but you're Restrained!
We're insane, but you're Restrained!
"We're insane, but you're Restrained!
[The voice picks up its tempo.]
We're insane, but you're Restrained!
We're insane, but you're Restrained!
We're insane, but you're Restrained!
No one cares.
No one cares.

RESIDENT
[*Jumps to his feet, and grabs the noose with both hands screaming.*]
Nooooooooooo!
[*He places the noose around his neck.*]

[DISENGAGE REVERB AND STROBE LIGHT]

[*Stage lights dim. SCENE curtain closes.*]

END OF ACT ELEVEN

ACT TWELVE

The stage is set with the white three-walled enclosure. There is a dummy, made up to resemble the Resident suspended in the middle of the set by means of the orange and green entwined rope and noose around its neck.

The hands of the stage clock turn to: 12 O'CLOCK.

The SCENE curtain opens. The stage lights are brought up. The stage is devoid of actors.

The voice on the public address system erupts.

VOICE

All Sirs...Madam...Inmate...Prisoners will be issued rose-tinted sunglasses!

[*A few moments after the public announcement all of the actors, with the exception of the Resident and the Priest, walk on to the stage from the wings wearing sunglasses. They mill about bumping into one another, but never touch the figure hanging from the rope - nor do they acknowledge its presence.*]

[ENGAGE REVERB AND WHITE STROBE LIGHT]

[*Sirens begin to wail, a red stage light begins to flash, and the actors pick up the pace of their movements. The PRIEST walks on stage from the left wing, and makes his way through the chaos. He is wearing rose-tinted sunglasses, and reading from The Bible. When he comes to the corpse of the hanged Resident, he closes The Book and removes his sunglasses to visually examine the hanged man. His examination completed, the PRIEST looks out at the audience and proceeds to walk to the front-center of the stage beyond the SCENE curtain. The pandemonium on the stage ceases, as does the siren and the flashing red light.*]

[DISENGAGE STROBE LIGHT.]

[*Silence ensues for a brief moment. The cast members on stage remove their sunglasses, and face the audience.*]

PRIEST

[*In a loud inquisitive voice, points a finger at the audience.*]
Thy will be done?

[*He looks back at the hanging man, then back at the audience. He replaces his sunglasses on his face, and exits stage right silently reading from The Bible.*]

[*The cast put their sunglasses back on, and mill about the stage as before. The red light flashes, and the siren resumes its wailing. The hands on the stage clock begin to turn counter-clock-wise. It is rewinding itself. Screams of torment, and cries of the baby can be heard, as the stage lights dim and engulf the stage in darkness. The noise of the pacing actors stops, replaced by the loud sound of the stage clock rewinding. Suddenly, the stage lights come on. The stage is empty, except for the hanging figure suspended by the rope. The mechanical winding becomes louder.*]

[*The SCENE curtain closes slowly.*]

[*Unexpectedly, the RESIDENT bursts through the closed SCENE curtain, and lunges at the stage clock. He is dressed in a white jumpsuit and sneakers, with a red "R" stamped upon his forehead. The orange and green noose is around his neck, with the rope itself extending through the closed SCENE curtain from behind him.*]

RESIDENT

[*Grabs the hands of the stage clock in panic, restricting the clock from rewinding itself, and he screams.*]
No more!

[*The stage curtain closes. The theme music from Kubrick's* A Clockwork Orange *is played through the public address system for a few minutes, with the repetitive skip at the third measure.*]

END OF PLAY

EPILOGUE

THE SEARCH

They looked for me
as they searched for me before
(I was retrieved)
through centuries passed,
which I have no living
recollection of.

They looked for me
on the plain
within the jungle
in the woods
upon the grasslands
on the prairie
in the rainforest.

They looked for me
to grow their plant
ation/rotation of their crop,
seeds from the Fertile Crescent
and of the fertile valleys,
too engorged by the corner-sewer's appetite...
too fat to satisfactorily feed itself.

They bound me
as the nanny
as the field hand
as the house nigger
as the railroad worker
as the inventor
as the innovator
as the nation builder
within a ship/meant
for the original ameriklan colonies...
as bountiful tribute
to England,

a predilection of 2½ centuries
as chattel circa 1641 Massachusetts.
Blind, due to out-sight,
inhumanity could not see me
as a true man.

They still look for me
in economically
socially
culturally
structurally (re)depressed ameriklan cities:
Roxbury
Cleveland
Detroit
Patterson
Brooklyn
Watts—
the public
private prison industrial's
complex service-related economy.

They desperately look for me
to fend off the hunger
to nourish their children
upon the carrion of my subsistence...
as a stepping stone
an inflated growth statistic
a natural resource
a profit margin.

Yesterday is today.

They look for me
(for their pleasure)
before I am born.

ABOUT THE AUTHOR

Ralph C Hamm III

Ralph, born in 1950, is serving a non-capital first offense life sentence for "intent," stemming from a criminal episode that occurred in 1968—when he was seventeen years old. During his decades of imprisonment he has aided in spearheading Massachusetts' prison reform movement, has earned degrees in liberal arts, divinity, metaphysics, and paralegal; as well as developed into a published poet, playwright, musician, and artist. In 2007 he was acknowledged as a contributor to the book, *When the Prisoners Ran Walpole* by Jamie Bissonette; and is author of *Manumission: The Liberated Consciousness of a Prison(er) Abolitionist*. Recently *The Tinderbox* (2013) and *Dear Stranger / The Wayfarer* (New Edition: 2014) were published by Little Red Cell Publishing, New London, CT.

CPSIA information can be obtained at www.ICGtesting.com
Printed in the USA
BVOW06s1611150915

417958BV00003B/22/P